The Business Side of Show Business

How to Make a Living Onstage

Caroline Ravn

struggle in their performing careers. It's full of great, practical, step-by-step advice on how to manage your career from the starting line to the stage in the modern era. Easy to read, with easy-to-understand lessons, from one of the great magicians of our time. Highly recommended!
Malcolm Larri, Public Speaker and Coach

I love this book! It has all the best business advice you would get in ten years of your own experience — or you could simply read this book. Caroline is super-honest, and it is awesome to read that. Awesome job, Caroline!
Wes Barker, Magician

There is a multitude of books about what tricks to do, but few are about how to make a living doing them. Caroline makes that information direct and easy to grasp. She's always impressed me with her consistent action toward achieving her goals, and you should act now and buy her book.
Bruce Gold

A thorough, in-depth look at the 101s of being a self-employed entertainer. Ravn shares her experience in a very digestible and condensed manner. It's all in here. This should be required reading for anyone looking to dive into show business. Essential tools to get started, and tips to level up working pros.
Leah Rose Orleans

The Business Side of Show Business

How to Make a Living Onstage

Caroline Ravn

BUSINESS BOOKS

London, UK
Washington, DC, USA

CollectiveInk

First published by Business Books, 2025
Business Books is an imprint of Collective Ink Ltd.,
Unit 11, Shepperton House, 89 Shepperton Road, London, N1 3DF
office@collectiveink.com
www.collectiveink.com
www.collectiveink.com/business-books

For distributor details and how to order please visit the 'Ordering' section on our website.

ISBN: 978 1 80341 959 6
978 1 80341 960 2 (ebook)
Library of Congress Control Number: 2024945957

A CIP catalogue record for this book is available from the British Library.

Design: Lapiz Digital Services

UK: Printed and bound by CPI Group (UK) Ltd, Croydon, CR0 4YY
Printed in North America by CPI GPS partners

We operate a distinctive and ethical publishing philosophy in all areas of our business, from our global network of authors to production and worldwide distribution.

Contents

Opportunity is missed by most people because it is dressed in overalls and looks like work.

— Thomas A. Edison

For my dad.
Thank you for always believing in me, driving me to gigs in places we didn't know existed, and offering to pay when we went grocery shopping together during my first year in business. I promise I won't tell my siblings.
Oh, sh*t!
All jokes aside, I owe you my whole life. Nothing will ever be the same now that you're gone. I will love and miss you forever.

The Journey of a Lifetime

You're currently reading the book I wish I'd had in hand when I started my business ten years ago. I knew where to find the tricks, how to get stage experience, and who to ask if I needed a special glue that would do a very specific thing – but I had no one to ask about how to make my passion my living.

You have too many tricks. There, I said it! Now we can move on to what matters.

All jokes aside, I will make a qualified guess: You have more tricks in your repertoire than you'll ever get to use in this or any upcoming lifetime. You bought books, lecture notes, and effects that you never opened. The tricks you perform are tricks you've done for a while – maybe for many years. You're happy with them. You may even have a show or act ready.

But you don't have a clear business plan, a thriving career, and a balanced life. You're not sure where and when the next show is coming from, and you don't know how to make a sustainable living doing what you love most.

If this sounds anything like you, this book is for you.

This book will cover zero magic tricks. I know this will disappoint a few of you, but I want to clarify that early on. You won't find any magic-related secrets at all here. There are too many other books with great (and not-so-great) material.

You already know your selected tricks, have gathered performing experience, and have sat through countless lectures. Now it's time to focus on *the business side of show business*.

As I write this, I'm sitting by the pool at a five-star hotel in Egypt. The kids are playing, the sun warms my face, and the coffee is just right. My business's tenth anniversary is coming up in a few weeks, and I can't help but reflect on all my decisions to get me to this point.

It's been a heck of a journey, from theology school and preaching to selling my soul to Satan for card tricks. I'm not saying it was easy; none of this was! However, it was worth it. I hope this book inspires you to go on a journey of a lifetime, look back ten years from now, and be proud of what you did.

Now it's time. I hope you're ready. Please enjoy, and thank me later.

Caroline Ravn

Part One
Foundations

This book is divided into different parts. I've tried to make all the parts and chapters stand alone so you can either read the book as written or use it as a reference book.

To start this off, I want to talk about essential foundations that will come in handy later. I didn't have all this set up when I first started, but I've found that it's a million, more or less, times better to have these things done and build on top of that. As I'm on a mission to make your life and journey more manageable than mine, I think this is an excellent place to start.

The foundations will be covered in two steps: The first focuses on your offer foundation, and the second on your business. Both are important and will require time and effort to implement.

I'm going to assume you already have a show or act of some sort to sell. If you don't, the best way to get something to offer your clients is to get a lot of stage time quickly. You get that through free gigs, comedy clubs, and improvisation ("improv") stages. Enjoy the process — it makes it more doable.

Let's build your foundations, shall we?

Your Offer Foundation

When talking to potential clients and later booking gigs, you want to have a few things prepared. These must be ready to lay a good foundation for your "offer" (which will be your show for most readers).

I've seen too many entertainers sit around with terrible websites, old pictures, and no promotional ("promo") material. Getting an act booked out of nowhere or with terrible marketing isn't likely to happen. Don't let that be you. Take control of your career and increase the likelihood of someone booking you to their event.

Some entertainers seem to think it's enough to be talented and do a "good enough" show. If they are "good enough," some manager will find them and give them all they ever dreamt of. I'm sorry to tell you this, but that won't happen for most of us.

Clear Offers

What's your product? What type of events do you perform at? Knowing what to tell a client about your show is crucial in the initial communication.

I used to be a "generalist." I would take on all the gigs that came my way. Now, my offers are precise, and I'm only doing what I'm good at. When you know your offers, writing copy and sales texts for them becomes much more manageable.

Get a piece of paper, or open a document on your computer or phone. Write down your offers and explain them in one sentence or a maximum of two sentences. Circle two of them that you enjoy and do really well. Those will be your core offers. I offer all parts of my list, but I always start pitching my core offers.

Here's my list:

- Closeup show
- Closeup walkaround magic
- Trade shows
- Stage show (20–90 minutes)
- Cruise shows
- Emceeing
- Public speaking
- Commercials/content creation for brands

My core offers are emceeing and a 25-minute stage show. What are yours?

Pricing

Don't guess how much money the client might have and then set your price. Set the price for your offers according to your skill level and experience. In the beginning, it will probably not be a lot, but with experience and the right framing, the price will go up. I usually change my pricing once a year.

So, when sending out your offers, know how much they cost. You can always offer discounts or package deals, but I encourage you to stay at the price you decided on and add more value if there are objections.

If the client can't go up to match your fee, *they* might be the party to go up in value. Meaning, what can they add on their end to bring up the value for you? Things that are valuable for magicians are usually pictures, videos, press, newsletters, and repeat bookings.

Pictures

Headshots

I don't know what it is with magicians really, but many seem to think that the best pictures are the ones where they look terrified and surprised, pointing either at playing cards or at a magic wand. This is not what you want.

Instead, try putting the same energy into the pictures you do as when you are doing what you're offering. Give the prospective client the full experience when it comes to your energy and charm. If they don't know you and haven't seen you already, it's very hard to get a feel of what you do from a picture where you're pointing at something you're not using and looking surprised while doing so.

Action shots

This is you in full action, doing what you offer. If you're offering a stage show, take great stage pictures. If you're doing trade shows, you want photos of people in a booth, with you performing or laughing, and the audience engaged.

For walkaround you want pictures of you doing something interesting with delighted people watching you do that. The focus is on the reaction, not on you doing the magic.

A bonus here is to get as many different versions of your action shots as possible. This will come in handy when selling to different industries. It's easier to sell if the people in the picture look like the prospective client. That means you need pictures with you and laughing children if you want to sell a kids' show. If you want to do fancy cocktail parties, take pictures when people are dressed up for that occasion.

At high-end events, especially corporate events, there will be a hired photographer. This person is in the same position as you — they want to do a good job. Instruct the photographer on what makes a good magic reaction picture. Most audience volunteers will also be okay with staging a little to make the picture better. When you see the photographer say, "Oh, here's the photographer! Look like I just blew your minds!" And most of the time, they will react accordingly. Don't underestimate the power of asking.

Venue shots

This is very close to action shots, but it's you on the kind of stage you're looking to sell a show for. If you're looking to get your show booked for a gala show, there's a big difference between showing a picture of you standing on the floor with 13 kids sitting in front of you, and one of you on a well-lit stage in front of 800 guests. If you need new pictures, put yourself in a situation where that's possible, even if it's for "free." (More on that later.) Just getting those pictures, if they turn out great, is priceless.

Videos

If the client doesn't know you and is coming in cold, they might want to see you in action. As often as you can, bring a camera to your gigs to film yourself. You'll want a showreel that showcases you as the talent and the ideal audience for the event you're pitching for.

Remember that the audience's reaction is more important than your super-expensive, fancy-looking prop. When putting your showreel together, put yourself in the booker's shoes:

- What is the one thing they want to solve by bringing a magician to the event?
- What can you put into the video that showcases, in the best and quickest way, the outcome of bringing you in for their event?
- Try to keep the reel under a minute if possible.

Reviews

When a potential client contacts you about an event that you know you'll be an excellent fit for, don't be afraid to tell them about other events like the one they're presenting. Share some reviews and quotes from other clients who were happy with your services. The closer that event is to the one this new client seeks, the better.

If you're new to asking for reviews, you can always include one as a draft for the client. Initially, I followed up with my clients by email after the event, including a suggested quote to put on my website. It could look something like this:

> Hi [first name],
>
> Thank you so much for having me at your event the other day. I had a blast — what a crowd!
>
> I'd love to share this experience with upcoming clients. Could I ask you for a short review to put on my website? Maybe something like, 'Caroline Ravn was the perfect fit for our gala dinner! She brought up our CFO on stage — his mind is still blown! Highly recommend!'
>
> Let me know what works for you!
>
> All the best,
> Caroline

Contract and Riders

A contract doesn't need to be long and complicated. You can use ChatGPT to write one for you if you prompt it with the names of both parties, dates, what's agreed on, and so on. My first contracts were about half a page long. Now, they come with my technical riders, emcee introduction, and all sorts of sheets.

What matters is that you have a contract template ready for when the show gets booked. Make it easy to change a few things (name, date, type of event, and so on). Let it grow with you over time. Having the template ready will reduce a lot of stress and save you loads of time.

Bio

In short, your bio is a mini-biography that answers the question: Who are you as an entertainer? What do you offer? Make this text exciting, and go big. What are the most incredible things you've done? What's most exciting about you?

Here's my bio:

> Caroline Ravn is one of the world's foremost female magicians.
>
> Early in her career, she won awards in the Swedish and Nordic Magic Championships. She was named Inspirational Person of the Year and received the prestigious Truxa Award for her remarkable achievements both nationally and internationally.
>
> She has been invited to perform at TEDx events on five separate occasions and is a regular headliner on luxury cruise ships worldwide.
>
> Her show, which is a delightful blend of humor and magic, has taken her from the town of Höganäs in the south of Sweden to the Mecca of magicians: Las Vegas.

Show Descriptions

This is similar to your core offer sentences, but here, you can go deeper. Describe the feelings and thrills of the shows and offers. There is no need to mention the tricks you're performing, but explain the show as grandly as possible.

A text like that will be perfect to send to agents so they can easily forward the texts to potential clients.

Agents and Managers

Know that most agents and managers take 30% of your income. If you want someone to help you get clients, you have to be ready to pay for it. Many also charge an hourly fee for meetings, scheduling, and planning.

I've worked with my agent since 2017; she takes 30%. She's my closest partner in crime and my best business friend. You want someone on your side who wants what's best for you.

Where do you want to spend your time? Is there something you don't like doing that can be outsourced? If you're uncomfortable making cold calls and actively promoting yourself, 30% isn't much to pay for someone to get you a gig.

Show Lengths

Shows vary depending on the audience. Especially if you're dealing with people coming up and down from the stage multiple times. Some want to play along, some may not want to be there, and some might even try to take over. However, here are some guidelines to consider when creating your offers:

- Show lengths for corporate shows: 20 minutes, 30 minutes, and 45 minutes are usually good marks. My preferred length is 25 minutes, and that's usually the perfect time for me for an after-dinner show.
- If you're looking to do cruises, you'll need two completely different 45-minute shows and sometimes an extra 20 minutes for a variety show. If you dream of being a cruise entertainer, you're looking at a fun lifestyle if you like to travel. The benefits include good, consistent money for nine months of the year, getting paid to see the world, and having loads of time for yourself. The downside is that you're dead to the rest of the world and live in a cabin. I balance it by doing just a few cruise contracts every year.
- Theater shows for tours and one-offs are usually 75–90 minutes long. If the show is longer than 75 minutes, an intermission is usually recommended.
- Variety and comedy clubs vary a little, but a really tight 6–12-minute act is always good to have.

- TEDx talks are a maximum of 18 minutes, but aim for 15.
- TV spots should be as short and to the point as possible. Depending on the show and segment, they usually want a visual lasting 3–5 seconds, 1 minute, or 3 minutes depending on the spot. I did a 16-minute interview once, but that's extremely rare!

Costume and Hygiene

I wish I didn't have to type these words, but here we go: Please wear clean clothes and shoes. Take showers regularly, and preferably before every gig. Use deodorant. Clean your hands and do a simple manicure from time to time. Yes, this goes for all the men too! It's not that hard to look and smell your best.

You don't need to buy expensive suits to look like the pro you're trying to portray. In fact, the dress I wear most often as an emcee only cost me $15 and has served me well!

I know you love your playing card shirts and ties, but they must stay in the closet. Corporate shows, weddings, and most private parties prefer elegance and class over humoristic clothing.

If you walk around in heels, I recommend staying clear of cheap leather. They're going to look like crap, feel even worse, and you'd be better off in flats.

I wear heels onstage, but the following advice goes for everyone wearing shoes onstage: Use a sports stick or cream to ease the pressure on your toes. Onstage, you're likely to sweat and swell a little, and you want to be as comfortable as you can. I use Active Anti Friction Balm from The Skin Agent.

You have a massive advantage over most other magicians when all this is done. With this solid foundation set in place, it's time to start building your successful business.

Your Whys and Your Goals

Why do you want to make this work for you? Only you can answer that — and your answer should be as detailed as you can make it. There will be times that are crazy hard and days when you want to quit and return to whatever you did before — go back to what was safe and familiar. On those days, you'll be happy that you took the time to think this through.

What are you currently sitting with? This is the first thing you must consider before doing anything. You will be your own boss and manage your time, part-time or full-time. I've seen too many people who "make a living" without actually "living," and I wish I had known the difference sooner.

So, why do you want to do this? Why is it *important* to you? It's a huge question. It might seem like it doesn't matter much, but indeed it does.

Let's start with me so you can understand what this might look like for you.

It started with me as a 3-year-old little girl. I was the cutest thing living on this planet, I'm sure. One day, my grandfather began pulling coins from behind my ear. Classic! But that moment of wonder never left me. That's where magic started for me — 30 years ago.

The entrepreneur part has always been there. I was one of those kids and teenagers who never sat still. I still can't sit, even if I try. I even performed until I was 34 weeks pregnant with my twin boys — and got back onstage when they were 3 weeks old.

I was a bullied child and teenager. I never felt like I was fitting in anywhere. However, I always had a project I was working on, and it was easy to find my whys and goals. There was always a reason.

I feared sitting still and was also worried nobody would ever notice me. It is so sad when you think about it. Every day,

I felt that if I wasn't constantly moving, somebody would notice me or, even worse, not notice me. I was so insecure but still determined to make it – whatever that meant.

The "reason" for most people is that we are running away – either from or towards something. And I feel like, in my case, I ran away from something. I ran away from being lonely and being bullied. I ran from embarrassment. From shame.

Today, I'm not lonely. I'm super-happy and proud of where I am. I want to do something extraordinary for myself, and magic has been my output. I've always loved magic. It's been an essential part of my life for most of my life. But this whole entrepreneurship thing... When I started doing magic professionally, I had nobody to ask about that.

I wish I'd had someone to tell me how to write a contract. How do you find clients? Turns out that's a big one. To do this professionally, you want to ensure that people pay for your services. Just "essential" information, like how you set up a web page, would be excellent. How do you know if you should use your regular or stage name? How do you post something that looks professional on social media? Do you have to have Instagram? What the heck is LinkedIn, and who is it for?

My grandfather always told me that a magician's job is not to keep the secrets of magic *from* the audience but to keep it *for* them. I've now come to understand that he might have stolen that quote from someone. "Steal like an artist," I guess. No matter where it came from, the quote is beautiful.

For me, it's a dear memory of my grandpa. Let's leave it at that. He was such an inspiration to me. He made me feel so much childlike wonder. Unfortunately, he passed away a long time ago.

My why? I want to create the same feeling in my audience – just that one feeling: wonder.

Have you heard that most people only see one magician in their lives? If that's true, I want to ensure that if I'm that person,

I do the best possible show for them — not only for myself or for them but also for magic as an art.

That is what I want to do. That *matters* to me.

When it comes to being an entrepreneur, a business owner, or an industry leader, it's important to me to ensure that I'm helping other people. Let me give you an example of how I like to help in my local community.

I was invited to be on the panel for 200 kids just about to choose which high school to attend. Three people were on the panel: myself, a guy who worked with youngsters getting out of gangs, and a consultant for the city. I was the coolest one there, mainly after I had performed a trick.

They all loved it!

After a short interview, the room opened up for questions. All but one of the questions were for me. They wanted to know my salary, how much I charge for a show, and what it's like to travel when someone else is paying. It blew their minds! As I got all these questions, all I could think about was that I hoped I had inspired at least one of these 200 teenagers to go through high school with the goal of one day starting their own business, too.

I want to remind you that this wasn't always me. I always sat in the back, and nobody talked to me. I was picked last, if at all. Nobody wanted me on their team. I'm telling you now: You can do this too. If I could, so can you.

Now, let's move on to some goals.

My biggest goal is to host the Eurovision Song Contest. I know, the most incredible thing in the world! I absolutely can't wait for the day. They say it's the most magical show of the year. Why not have a magician host it? I'm volunteering!

I might change my mind tomorrow. I think I will stop performing weekly when I'm around 60. By then, I would love to work more with theater. Maybe as a theater director or consultant. The best thing about running your own business is that you can change your mind and be free to move in any direction.

Your goals can and will change over the years. Eight years ago I wanted to run away with the circus!

My goals used to include wanting to take over after Copperfield. I still want to be a Disney princess voice. I would prefer it in Swedish because I have a southern accent, and it's cute.

Write down your goals and your dreams. One of my favorite things with a goal is to write it down and backtrack.

What do you have to do to reach the goal? Let's take Eurovision, for example. How do I get there? The step right before Eurovision could be to host the Swedish version, where the viewers find the song that will represent Sweden in the contest. Another step before that is to present on that TV network. How can I make sure I'm an excellent TV personality? What can and should I do to ensure I'm sitting in a position where I can even be considered for a gig like that?

You have a dream. If you want to make it real, I'm telling you, you can. It's going to be hard work, but it's going to be worth it — so worth it.

So why do you want to do this? What do you dream about?

SMART(er) Goals

"SMART" stands for Specific, Measurable, Achievable, Relevant (or Realistic depending on which model you use), and Time-bound.

Setting clear and achievable goals is crucial in personal and professional development. The concept of SMART goals has become a cornerstone in this pursuit, providing individuals and organizations with a structured framework to enhance their goal-setting process.

Let's review the five aspects individually, and I'll share examples that I hope you'll find helpful.

Specific

Setting specific goals involves clearly defining what you want to achieve. If your objectives are vague, it's challenging to measure your progress and determine whether it was a success. But when a goal is specific, it provides a roadmap, guiding you towards a well-defined and known outcome. For instance, instead of setting a general goal like "I want to improve my fitness," a specific goal would be "I want to run 5 km in under 25 minutes." Or, in our case, a general goal would be "I want to shuffle cards better," and a specific one would be "I want to make a perfect faro shuffle."

Measurable

Measuring progress is crucial for staying on track and maintaining motivation. A measurable goal establishes concrete criteria for tracking your progress. In the fitness example, you can measure progress by tracking your running times or distances covered. This aspect allows you to celebrate achievements and make necessary adjustments if needed. In the faro shuffle example, it can be helpful to check how far "off" you were and see how small changes in the handling could help you improve and reach your final goal.

The final measurement would be to complete a 5-km run or make that perfect faro shuffle consistently.

Achievable

Goals should be challenging – but achievable! An achievable goal stretches your abilities without setting you up for failure. Consider your current skill set, available resources, and time constraints when setting your goals. Aiming for a gradual increase in difficulty ensures a sense of accomplishment and helps with continuous growth.

Doing a faro shuffle is challenging, but it can be done, so it's achievable.

Relevant

Relevance is about ensuring that your goals align with your overall objectives. A relevant goal contributes to your broader mission, making your efforts more purposeful. Before committing to a goal, ask yourself if it truly matters in the context of your personal or professional journey. If you're a corporate magician, for example, it might not be super-relevant to take a week to focus on balloon twisting. However, adding emceeing to your packages might be a relevant goal.

Time-bound

Time-bound goals come with a specific timeframe for completion. In the past, I've used magic competitions for this. I've found that it's much easier to stay focused and on track with a goal if I have a hard deadline, like a competition or a specific event. I work well under pressure, and if you do too, it might be a good idea to have short deadlines to complete parts of a goal. That's the best way for me. If you don't know how to do your best work, try different boundaries and choose what works best for you moving forward.

Having SMART(er) goals has helped me stay on track, prioritizing when life gets busy and ensuring I'm doing the work I should be doing. For far too long, I didn't realize I was a procrastinator extraordinaire and that doing the laundry and the dishes, making the bed, and reorganizing the cupboards wouldn't get me anywhere. But my home was spotless. Spotless!

Creating a Business Plan

As far as setting your foundation goes, you're already well on your way. The next step is to write a business plan.

You have your goals. You have your whys sorted. But what is a business plan? And how do you create one?

I wish I had taken the time to sit down and write one when I got started. It would have saved me many headaches and so much time. Learn from my mistakes, and don't make the same ones. If you need to stop reading the book after this chapter to get it done, do so! The rest of the book will be here waiting. I promise!

I went all in, and I had no plan. I had no idea what I was doing. Let's make sure that you are better set than I was. Here are some questions and headlines to help you in this process.

What Is Your Business Idea?

What is it that you do? What does your business offer others? My business is that I perform magic. People buy my services for company parties such as corporate mingles, gala shows, or conferences. They hire me to do the entertainment.

So you have to think about what it is that you do. Are you a magician also for hire? Maybe an emcee? Public speaker? Are you a content creator offering other companies exposure on your platforms?

Our next step in this process is to think about our vision.

What Do You Want to Achieve?

As I said earlier, I want to create a feeling of wonder in my audience. That's important to me and something I strive for in all my shows.

In this part of the business plan, you also add your goals. This should be easy now that you've set them in the earlier chapter. Are your goals SMART?

What problems do you see your business solving?

If you're looking to be on prestigious stages, it might be an idea to write down "cruises," "TEDx talks," or anything like that into your vision.

What do you want to be known for? How does that question make you feel? What gets you excited?

Where will you be one, three, five, and ten years from now? This part of your business plan should be reviewed a few times a year. I do mine at the start of every quarter. I advise you to do the same.

Clients and Markets

Where do you offer and sell your services? Who are your customers? Which group or groups are you targeting? What, if any, purchasing power do they have?

I mainly work with agents and event planners now. They usually come with a bigger budget. However, if you're starting and don't have any agents or event planners in your network yet, I would go for HR (Human Resource) managers, executive assistants, and office managers for corporate shows, and busy parents for family parties.

Think about these clients and their problems. What's keeping them up at night? What can you do to solve their problems?

Why are you that person for them? The clearer you can be on this, the easier for you to reach out to these people.

Where and in Which Industry Do You Work?

How big is your market? How do you see it changing over the next five to ten years?

I mainly do more significant events. It's not often that I mingle anymore or go to private parties. My market is corporate shows, primarily with an audience of over 120 people.

Competition

Who else is in your market? What do they do, and what do their offers look like? What can you learn from them? Are you just performing locally, or do you travel to other places? What kinds of performers are in those places? What are their strengths and weaknesses?

Look at what they're doing right and "steal like an artist." Get inspired by them, but don't steal any copy from their websites. You want to be seen as a co-worker, not a total a**hole. The magic industry is small, and words travel fast.

Product and Service

What is your Unique Selling Point (USP)? Are you the product? Is the product adaptable to the customer's needs?

My product is me. I am the show. I'm a woman in a male-dominated industry, which makes me unique just by that fact alone. But I don't only want to be "the woman magician," so I've added "five-time TEDx speaker and emcee" and made my show a combination of comedy and magic. I've also worked hard to be a cruise magician, which gives me a lot of credibility when being picked for bigger audiences.

On top of that, I do my show in two languages (Swedish and English) and can switch between them if needed. In my show, I invite the audience to have a peek into my personal life to make me more relatable.

I was marketing myself as "the leading female magician in Sweden," but a while back, I changed this to "one of the leading magicians in Sweden."

What makes you unique?

Business Model

Which price level do you have? How does that compare to the competitors in your market? Is the price per hour, event, or something else? How do you sell it?

How do you get paid? Do you take deposits or retainers when signing a contract? Do you send the invoice after the show and add all extra costs, such as travel, on top of the fee?

Do you accept PayPal, cash, or credit cards?

I send my invoices after the shows and add pre-agreed extra costs associated with the event.

Legal Structure

Every country has different laws and structures. Look into the different ones you have in yours, and ask an accountant and a tax representative for more critical knowledge.

The business structures in Sweden come with various prices, benefits, and risks. The one I have now is called an AB.

Analysis

What are your business's strengths and weaknesses? What opportunities do you see for your business now and in the future? Is there anything you need to consider regarding possible threats to your company?

What are the pros and cons of keeping your name and having a stage name? What will this do to you in the future? My name was legally changed to my stage name, Caroline Ravn, before I became a full-time magician. Now that I'm somewhat famous, I wish I had kept my original surname, Nilsson, to make my private life more private.

Budgeting

Now let's talk about money.

Before I had a budget, I would look into my personal and business accounts and say, "Ooh, money in the account – lovely!" or "Oh no, no money. I hope Dad's cooking today so I can go there for dinner."

If you're looking to do magic part-time, budgeting might not be something you have to do right now. If the money is just nice-to-have and not need-to-have, leave this chapter for now.

But if you want to make a full-time living doing magic, you will want to be able to take out a salary and save for the future. You'd have to ask an accountant how this would work.

When creating a budget, you will look at all costs and sources of income associated with your business. This includes salary, insurance, taxes, travel, props, conventions, and so on. It should also take into account money for shows, sponsorships, and sales of merchandise ("merch").

If you've had your business for a while already, the easiest way to go about this would be to go through your bank account, see the numbers, and add them to the budget. Aim for at least three months, but preferably an entire year. Judging and questioning your decision is easy the first time you do this. Try not to do that, then add the numbers in. Knowing where the money goes is the first step in making better decisions.

What are you going to spend the money on? Are you going to take out a salary every month? Will it be the same every month? Will you have an office, or will you work from home? Do you need to buy a new computer? Do you need any fancy software? There are a bunch of different tools that you might want to invest in and ads you'd probably want to run. I don't think you need more magic props or books for now.

Making magic a living requires a lot of sacrifice. You'll experience busy months and slow seasons. A pandemic might hit you again! Think about the life you want and try your best to create a realistic budget that supports that vision.

In my case, I have a partner, two kids, an apartment, and a house we're planning on bringing down to make space for a much bigger one. I have to take out a high salary so that I'll be able to get a loan from the bank to help with the build.

Money and budgeting could be a book on their own! The tools I use to have an overview are Google Sheets, my accounting and invoice program Fortnox, and regular meetings with my accountant. There, we review the financial situation, plan taxes, and plan for the future.

I also used to have yearly meetings with my bank manager, but I don't need them anymore. Most banks offer these services for free to their paying business clients. See what your bank offers to see if it makes sense to you. That said, I have a few different bank accounts. One group is just for private finances, and the other is just for my business.

I divide my income into different parts depending on where the money comes from. In my case, a typical month includes magic shows, emcee gigs, merchandise sales, affiliate deals, and consultations. On average, in 2023, I brought in about $17,000 per month. In the low season it was less, and around the holidays it was more. Since I want to spend as much time as possible with my twin toddlers, I've turned down a lot of work over the past two or three years.

My expenses in a typical month are usually my salary, office, agents, staff, taxes, insurance, Google Ads, and phone bill. I pay for some services monthly but prefer to pay yearly for things I love and use. For higher rates, I always try to get a yearly price because it's usually much cheaper.

Remember, I've done this for a while, so my numbers will be higher than for many of you. My services start at $2500 and range up to $9000. My starting price ten years ago was $150, and I had very low costs.

Plan for future costs. Always have a set budget for marketing and generating leads. If money is tight, use it on showreels and social proof, not a new and shiny trick.

Time Management

For most entrepreneurs and business owners, time management isn't just a skill; it's a component of success.

As magicians, we wear many hats: performer, marketer, business manager, and more. Juggling these roles effectively requires discipline, organization, and a strategic approach to managing our time.

One of the most important principles of time management is prioritization. Since time is limited, it's essential to identify your most important tasks and use it accordingly. Whenever I doubt what to do next, I ask myself: What money-making activity can I do right now? It usually gives me insight into my next move.

If you are your own boss, you genuinely need this skill. What do you want to achieve in your magic career? Whether booking more gigs, mastering a new sleight, or expanding your online presence, clearly defined goals will guide your prioritization when it comes to your time.

I've heard too many magicians say things like, "Oh, it must be lovely to be a full-time magician. You can sit around all day and then go do the gig at night and make loads of money." The money is excellent, but I rarely "sit around." I'm running a business. I'm a small business owner. I'm an entrepreneur.

Set your working hours and try to stick with them. That said, I work a lot of nights and weekends, too. I love running my business. Just like I love magic, I now have two dream jobs in one. Yay me!

Remember that not all tasks are equal. Focus on activities that directly contribute to your goals and generate the most value (usually money) for your business. For magicians, this might include practicing new routines, networking with potential clients, or creating promotional materials for your shows. Most of the time, it means selling your show.

Time blocking is a powerful technique for managing your schedule and maximizing productivity. By allocating specific blocks of time to different activities, you can minimize distractions and ensure that you progress on your most important stuff. Here's how you can implement time blocking in your magic business.

Scheduled Practice

Dedicate regular blocks of time to practicing your magic and performance skills. This could be running over your script, working on a routine, or testing new movements between effects.

Email Habits

Find a good emailing schedule that fits you and your work hours. It's so easy to check your email and social media platforms constantly, but try to limit your access to them. I've found it helpful to remove all unnecessary distractions from my phone, such as notifications and my screen lighting up.

Rather than checking your email constantly throughout the day, set aside dedicated blocks of time. This will help you avoid distractions and maintain focus on your other things. For me, it works best to do emails four times every day. When I get to the office, I clear up everything as if it was a to-do list. Before I go to lunch, I check for anything that needs my attention, then again after lunch. Both times, it's mainly a check-in. If something is urgent, I usually handle it directly. If it's not urgent, I handle it before I leave the office at the end of the day.

Find what works for you. I'm not trying to be a drama queen here, but take control of your inbox, or it might take control over you.

Social Media Habits

I'm all for scrolling endlessly on Instagram. Honestly, I enjoy being sucked into a rabbit hole and not knowing how I ended up there. But not on my work time. Sometimes, I'm looking for inspiration for a post or video, but then I head in with my research goggles on.

Social media is a valuable tool for marketing your magic business, but it can also be a significant time sink if you're not careful. Set boundaries around your social media usage and avoid getting sucked into endless scrolling. Consider using social media scheduling tools to plan and automate your posts. (More on that later. Or should I say, "More on that *Later*"? You'll get it — Later.)

Multitasking

While it may seem efficient to manage multiple projects and tasks simultaneously, research has shown that multitasking decreases productivity and impairs cognitive function. Instead of trying to do everything at once, focus on one task at a time and give it your full attention.

When I can, I like to have dedicated days for things when I have a lot in motion. I might dedicate entire days to filming, writing, or rehearsing something. That way, it's a full day of something in particular; it's easier for me to stay focused and not get lured into doing everything at once.

Procrastination

We've all been guilty of putting off essential tasks in favor of more enjoyable activities. To overcome procrastination, break your tasks into smaller, more manageable chunks and tackle them individually. Set deadlines for yourself and hold yourself accountable to ensure that you stay on track.

There's a book I highly recommend to everyone: *The War of Art* by Steven Pressfield. It's about The Resistance and how we can overcome it. Do yourself a favor and read it twice a year. It's a short read but incredibly transforming.

Your USP

When a client is planning an event and thinks about hiring a magician, what's the first thing they do? Most likely, they start googling (I love how that's a word — in your face, Bing). What sets you apart from someone else if they get to your website? What makes you the better, or even more interesting, choice?

Take some time to figure out your USP — your Unique Selling Point. Make it memorable and easy to explain in one sentence. To start, think of your favorite magicians and explain them in one sentence. You could even ask your friends and family if you're ready to hear what they say. My sister is my most prominent critic, so I only ask her on really good days. All-stars-aligned, slept-well, and my-mental-health-is-intact days.

Stack your strengths and talents. Where are you different from others? Is it in the type of performance you do, what you look like, or how you bring people up onstage? Try to dig into where you stand, and exemplify what makes you unique. Maybe you're the closeup guy or the illusion dudette.

It can also help to look into your business plan for this and see your target audience in front of you when trying to explain your USP. What need are you filling?

Be clear about who you are rather than trying to be a one-size-fits-all solution. You can position yourself as an expert in your field by having a clear niche. That's much easier if you're not a generalist.

Your personality and style as a performer can also be a key component of your USP. Are you charming and charismatic, or mysterious and enigmatic? Do you have a signature look or catchphrase that sets you apart from other magicians? Embrace what makes you unique as a performer and incorporate it into your performance identity. Remember, clients aren't just hiring you for your magic tricks; they're hiring you for the experience and entertainment value you bring to their event.

Finding your Unique Selling Point as a magician is a process of self-discovery and self-expression. By identifying your strengths, understanding your audience's needs, and embracing what makes you unique as a performer, you can develop a compelling USP that sets you apart from the crowd and attracts clients to your magic business. So embrace what makes you unique.

It took me years to figure out who I was, so it's not an easy afternoon tea assignment. Let it evolve and come to you over time.

Part Two
Your Tools

I want to make my business operation as smooth as possible, especially now that I have toddlers at home. During the hours when I'm not performing or needing to work either *on* or *in* the business (there's a big difference), I'm trying to be as present as possible with the kids. Therefore, I'm constantly trying to ensure that all parts of my business are as self-contained and self-working as possible. Your time and energy are resources you'll want to pay extra attention to. Create structures to help you stay on track so you can do all the fun stuff without risking burnout because of all the admin that comes with running a business.

You're reading this book to take a more serious approach to your entertainment business. There are a few things you'll want to have sorted to make your life a little easier. These are tools I use, and they make sense to me. They might not be the best for you, but I've added them here for full transparency.

I recommend that you start with one piece at a time. At least once a year, I take the time to overview my operation to see what's missing, what's working, and what isn't. I look at what I'm enjoying doing and what I can outsource.

Most of the tools and programs I use today are paid versions to get all the needed benefits. However, most of them also come with free versions or trials. Try using the free versions before buying anything! If you can't find a free version offered on the site, I would email their customer service and see if there's a way to get a trial to see if it's a good fit.

Don't pay for anything you don't need, and don't spend your time (and money) doing the wrong thing. I hope this helps. The same goes for new magic tricks — I can't stress that enough.

Website

To communicate what I do, I have a few different websites. My main website is www.carolineravn.com, and I send most potential clients and partners there. It has all my existing offers, press photos, blog posts, podcasts I've been a guest on, and more. That's usually the first step for clients who haven't seen me live. The website is connected to Google Ads, on which I spend about $1500 monthly. Most of my clients come in through my website.

My website is a living place where I stay consistent with new pictures, testimonials, and updates when something big happens.

I'm delighted with the design of my website. Before I could afford someone else to do it, I used WordPress and a free theme. It did the job just fine. I'm still using WordPress, and I find it easy enough to use. Other options for you to consider are Wix and Squarespace. I've seen and heard great things about both of them. One great thing about going with a big company that many are using is that there are usually hundreds if not thousands of instruction videos on YouTube.

For full transparency, the website I have now cost me around $6000, plus $2500 for pictures.

While having a visually appealing and user-friendly website is crucial for communicating your offers effectively, it's equally important to ensure that your website is optimized for search engines. SEO (Search Engine Optimization) plays a huge role in driving organic traffic to your website and maximizing its visibility in search engine results pages.

My main website, www.carolineravn.com, is the cornerstone of my online presence, acting as the primary destination for most people. By regularly updating my website with new content, such as blog posts, podcasts, and testimonials, I provide valuable information to visitors but also signal to search engines that my site is active and relevant.

Consistency is key when it comes to SEO. By regularly updating your website with fresh content, testimonials, and relevant keywords, you can improve your site's ranking in search results and attract more organic traffic — and that's what we want.

Investing in professional photographs for your website is another smart move, as high-quality images can enhance the overall aesthetics and credibility of your site. Incorporating descriptive alt text and captions for your images can also improve your website's accessibility and SEO performance. WordPress has a built-in service for checking this, and I'm sure other platforms offer that too.

While a visually appealing website is essential for engaging visitors and communicating your offerings effectively, integrating SEO into your website strategy is crucial for maximizing its visibility and attracting organic traffic. By staying proactive with your SEO efforts and leveraging the right tools and platforms, you can ensure that your website remains a powerful asset for bringing in the right clients.

I've seen many magicians' websites, and I think many of them aren't even considered by prospective clients, or even lose opportunities because of their websites. Have a look at your site and be honest with yourself: Would *you* book you?

Google Ads and Business

Establishing a strong online presence is essential for anyone looking to expand their reach and attract new clients. Google Ads and Google Business offer powerful tools and platforms that can help businesses enhance their visibility, attract relevant leads, and grow.

Google Business, formerly known as Google My Business, is a free and powerful tool that allows business owners to manage their online presence across Google Search and Maps. By claiming and optimizing your Google Business listing, you can ensure that your contact information, hours of operation, and customer reviews are accurate and up to date. Think about it: When was the last time you searched for something on Google, and what did you do next? I usually type in my keywords, hit enter, and go to the maps/business section of what I searched for. With Google Business, what's the place you take control over?

Having a well-optimized Google Business profile can significantly enhance your visibility, making it easier for potential clients to find and contact you. Additionally, Google Business listings often appear prominently in local search results, giving you an edge over competitors.

Google Ads provides a highly targeted advertising platform to reach potential clients actively searching for services. By creating compelling ad campaigns and targeting specific keywords related to magic performances for events, for example, you can ensure that your ads appear in relevant search results.

Connecting your website to Google Ads is a smart way to drive traffic to your site. If you don't know how to set it up, there are probably thousands of videos on YouTube to tell you how to. If you want to go one more step, consider hiring a Google Ads expert. I've seen success doing both.

One of the key advantages of Google Ads is its flexibility and scalability. You set your own budget and bidding strategy, allowing for precise control over advertising costs. Additionally, Google Ads offers robust analytics and reporting tools, enabling you to track the performance of the ads in real time and optimize campaigns for maximum effectiveness.

Email and Newsletters

I've tried many different emailing services. Some paid, some free. When I say many, I mean many. The one I've landed on is MailChimp. It's the easiest, most user-friendly tool (that actually works) that I've come across. It does all it needs to and gives me all the analytics that I need. I'm on a paid plan for it, but the free version worked for the first eight years.

Given my bilingual capabilities in Swedish and English, I have two main lists. Furthermore, I have segmentation based on the interests and preferences of subscribers. Whether they signed up through landing pages related to my book or are loyal customers of my playing cards, segmenting my lists allows me to tailor content and offers accordingly.

In managing my email communications, I use both my own domain email address and several Gmail addresses. This strategic approach helps me maintain organizational clarity, ensuring that emails are directed to the appropriate audience and inbox. It's basically like when people have a spam email address that they use for newsletters and such. Since my business and life have different areas, I divide the email addresses accordingly. Some email addresses are even used by team members.

To break it down to what you need, I'd say one email address that's for your business (like info@carolineravn.com) and some way of sending out newsletters. If you run different types of businesses, I would recommend you have separate email addresses and newsletter lists.

To make sure my grammar is okay and that I don't run into any awkward spelling errors when it matters, I'm using Grammarly. They have a great free version online, but I've used the paid version for a year or so to get the ability to change the tone of what I write. This is next level and should be very far down your list.

I write a lot of content such as newsletters, blog posts, guest articles, this book, and so on. Swedish is my first language, but English is a close second. Still, I've found it helps tremendously to have a spelling program installed that automatically checks my spelling, grammar, and phrasing.

Calendar and Calendly

I'm obsessed with a good calendar system. The one I've found to work the best is Google Calendar. I use different calendars within Google Calendar, and I use different colors to manage my life. One of the calendars in there is open to my agents and bookers. That way, they don't have to reach out to me before adding a potential booking to the calendar.

I also use it for notes and for planning where I need to be at what time. I time my reminders when I need to get ready to leave for important meetings. All notifications come to my computer, iPhone, and Apple Watch. The screen on my Apple Watch always shows what's next on my agenda.

If someone wants to book an appointment with me, I send them to my Calendly.

You know how we humans sometimes measure time, like before and after a specific event? Pre- and post-pandemic, for example. For my day-to-day business, that thing is Calendly.

Whenever I invite someone to a meeting, I send them a link to my Calendly that's connected and synced to my Google Calendar. If there's a slot free in my calendar – that is, during working hours I've set up in advance – someone can book an appointment with me in Calendly. Calendly will then send reminders, create a Zoom link for the meeting, and make sure it's added to my Google Calendar.

If it sounds like magic, it's because I'm pretty sure it is. If not that, it's like having a virtual assistant that reads your mind. So, magic.

Digital Meetings

In light of the digital shift brought on by the Covid-19 pandemic, I've wholeheartedly embraced the convenience and efficiency of Zoom for all my virtual meetings. As a dedicated Apple user, I've found Zoom to be particularly optimized for MacBooks and iPhones, making it my platform of choice for seamless communication.

Opting for a paid version of Zoom has allowed me to unlock more features and perks, including extended meeting durations and functionality, further elevating the quality of my meetings. It's a small investment that has made a significant difference in the professionalism and effectiveness of my digital meetings.

I've discovered several easy yet impactful ways to level up the quality of my Zoom meetings and enhance the overall experience for myself and my participants. I always get compliments for my setup and lighting!

One of the simplest upgrades is introducing additional light sources to improve visibility and clarity during video calls. Whether it's a desk lamp strategically positioned behind my device or a dedicated ring light, proper lighting can make a world of difference in how I'm perceived on camera.

Speaking of the cameras, I've invested in a 4K camera that I have set up in the office at all times. Another investment that I made was in a proper microphone. Now, the audio quality is amazing. It eliminates background noise and ensures that my voice comes through loud and clear.

It never hurts to look and sound (or smell) the best you can.

For those looking to take their Zoom meetings to the next level, integrating streaming software can add an extra layer of polish and professionalism. From overlaying graphics and text to incorporating music or sound effects, the possibilities for enhancing production value are endless. During the pandemic, I used Ecamm for this and was super-happy with it.

ChatGPT

This part of the book might reveal how dated it is before long. ChatGPT is an AI tool that's probably the best known as I'm writing this. It's a great tool for writing anything really, but also great for suggestions. I use it to come up with ideas for blog posts, LinkedIn posts, strategies for Instagram, and so on.

Try typing these prompts (the message you're giving the AI) and see the magic happen:

- Write ten subheadings for a blog post about magic on a cruise ship.
- Come up with five headlines to stop people from scrolling past my post about business advice for entertainers.
- Come up with a 30-day content plan for a small business owner who wants to get more engaging followers.

The uses of ChatGPT are endless. If you're ever running out of ideas, head over there to be inspired. I've created more ideas there than anywhere else – and I'm sure you will too! There's an art to writing good prompts. If you find it difficult, go to YouTube and dig up some good videos about it.

It's not perfect, but I asked ChatGPT to "Come up with five headlines to stop people from scrolling through my post about business advice for entertainers" and here's what I got back:

- "Unlock the Secret to Business Success: Essential Advice for Entertainers!"
- "Attention Entertainers: Transform Your Career with These Proven Business Tips!"
- "Don't Miss Out! Learn How to Turn Your Passion for Entertainment into Profit!"

- "Calling All Entertainers: Elevate Your Business Game with These Insider Secrets!"
- "Ready to Level Up? Discover Game-Changing Business Advice for Entertainers Today!"

Don't be surprised if you see me using some, if not all, of those headlines at some point.

Staying Organized

This can be summed up in one sentence, but I'll try my best to inspire you to think over your business organization before going rogue.

I use both Dropbox and Google Drive. Drive is for all my notes, courses, this book, YouTube ideas, and so on. Dropbox is shared with my agent, and that's where we keep all my contracts and my booking schedule. It sounds fancier than it is: It's basically an Excel document with name of event, contact person, fee, and date.

After the show, the same information gets moved over to another tab in the same document called "Past Clients." All my cue sheets and details for the event stay in Dropbox. It's all organized according to date.

The organization structure looks like this:

> Caroline Ravn AB – Upcoming Gigs – 20240112 Smart Optic – Notes, contracts, and sheets

If the client needs extra photos or videos, they go in the same folder.

After the show, the folder is moved to Caroline Ravn AB – Past Gigs. I want to keep all the notes if and when I get a repeat booking. It's always good to know which effects and services I've done for them before.

Some magicians use CRMs (Customer Relationship Management systems), but I prefer using Dropbox and Excel. My agent uses Pipedrive and is very happy with it. The most important thing is that you use something that makes sense to you.

Canva

My favorite content creation software, all categories, goes to Canva. It's a drag-and-drop idiot-proof Photoshop tool that takes your content to a new dimension within seconds.

Okay, that might be a little over the top, but it's a great tool to use for anything content-related. You can create business cards, banners, profile pictures, logos, and thumbnails, to name a few things. On a regular basis, I use it for YouTube thumbnails, email signatures, and Instagram posts. The paid version of Canva comes with a place to store your brand colors and fonts to make it easier to create something true to your brand.

I get a lot of questions about logos, brochures, and banners — what to put on them, how they should look, and so on. In 2024, I think that generally it's better to have an active social media presence, a good website, and a clear brand identity across all platforms.

Leave brochures and fliers as a thing of the past and move into a more digital space. Your money will most likely be wasted on paper, and the environment will thank you for staying digital. People search and consume online, so the money is best spent there.

Business Cards

Some of you may still use business cards, and they do have a place in most businesses. However, after receiving and handing out more business cards than I ever thought I'd see in a lifetime, I've changed my strategy.

I don't hand out or accept business cards anymore – unless I absolutely have to. They end up being thrown away, not used, and just a total waste. Instead, I'm using a QR code on my lock screen on my phone. Here's how I did it (but see an easier way right after).

I created a QR code with a free QR code creator service online. The QR code takes you to my LinkedIn profile. Then, I downloaded it and uploaded it to Canva. In Canva, I set the size of the project to be the same size as my phone. I inserted a picture I liked and put the QR code on top. I exported the picture, airdropped it to my iPhone, and made it my lock screen. *Voilà!* This took about four minutes to do.

Since then, you can now make this process even easier by just going to LinkedIn on your phone, pressing the search bar, and then there's a QR scanning toggle to your right. Press that, download just the QR code, and upload to Canva. Canva is also an app, so you can do the same process there.

When I talk to potential clients, I pull up my phone, they scan, and they are taken to my LinkedIn directly. You could also just open LinkedIn and press the QR toggle, of course, but I get distracted when I open my phone and see all the notifications pop up. I have my QR code on a few different pictures, so if I know there are a lot of mothers there, I make sure to have a picture with the twins. (I knew they would come in handy!)

It's extremely rare for me to hand out business cards these days, and when I do it's usually as part of a goodie bag. I like to have the client's info as well, and a reason to connect right away. LinkedIn is perfect for that.

What kind of business cards do you keep? Why do you keep them? I've heard event guests tell me that they saved business cards from certain magicians because the card had a prediction on it. They didn't use the word "prediction," but they have all been ecstatic when telling me how they got it, while pulling it out of their pocket.

Part Three
The Money Makers

Being a "professional magician" can mean a variety of things. Some people might want to do only closeup, and some only stage. Some might go all in with cruises, and some will do a few extra gigs here and there. Some might be magic-writers and some prop-builders.

In Part One: Foundations, I mentioned my offers and asked you to consider yours. In this part of the book, I'll walk you through some of the most common offers that you might have and give you some insight, in the widest strokes possible, into what I would recommend for you.

I'll also share what I would do, and usually do, for the given occasion. Some of you won't agree on this, but to be as helpful as I can, I figured I'd share it as inspiration. I'll help you think all the way for the first chapters and then let you fill in the blanks as we move along. Let's hope this doesn't get too confusing.

I don't have a lot of experience in residencies, so I wouldn't be much help in that regard. Therefore, there's only one experience of mine I can share. View it as a story more than advice. Here we go!

What to Charge

I don't think there's just one answer to this question, but many pros and hobbyists struggle with it. I can't tell you what you should charge, but there are a few factors I think should be considered before setting a price.

In general, I see that many performers are undercharged and don't see the value they provide. I hear magicians saying that they've heard what others in the area charge, and they want the gig, so they set a price just under that.

The fee will vary depending on whether you're a beginner, semipro, or professional. All of those can further be divided into how many shows you've done, if you're in demand, and how much money your target audience has to spend on the type of entertainment you're offering. Of course, the economy in the country you live in will be a factor as well.

To give you an idea of what it might look like, I'd like to share my fees for the first years into doing magic full-time:

- Walkaround: 1 hour $150; 2 hours $200
- Show: 20 minutes $300; 40 minutes $400

Today, my starting fee for closeup is $2500 and for shows $3000. My emcee fee starts at $4500.

I think it's important to see your worth, no matter the level you're at. Avoid doing things for free, and work for an exchange if there's no budget/payment.

Closeup

Many, if not most, magicians start with small tricks. My first trick was a rubber band trick, and my first card trick was a math trick. I uploaded a video of it on YouTube, asking if someone knew how and why it worked. Even with the explanation, I'm still not sure I understand it. But hey, it works!

Doing closeup magic can mean both doing a sit-down show, mingling magic, or magic during a dinner. No matter the situation, I'd like you to think of the performance as a show. That means the act should have a start, middle, and end.

For a show where you're seated at the table and the audience has been perfectly seated around you, so that all angles are protected, it's probably easier to do the show as intended.

When it comes to walkaround and mingling, your angles aren't always protected, nor can you control the situation the same way you could if they were, as in the arrangement above.

Here's what I usually do for a sit-down situation.

I'll have my chair on the long side of the table. The two short sides would have chairs by them, facing the audience more than me. So, sitting with an angle. For a 20-minute set, the outline of that show would be as follows.

Someone introduces me, and then I enter and talk to the audience a little before sitting down.

As I sit down, I'll share some stories about myself — the funnier, the better. I would use the line, "My grandfather was a magician, and my dad was a politician, so lying on the job was always encouraged." I would then sit during the laugh.

The first trick would be the jumping rubber band, and I would explain that that was where my magical journey started. I would then invite two volunteers to take the seats next to me.

Next would come Crazy Man's Handcuffs, introducing a deck of cards, a poker routine about chance, a triumph, a quick, ambitious card routine with literally one phase, and a little breather with a story about my twins and how I performed magic for the midwives and doctors during labor and how that went viral. Then I would do a sandwich routine, where I find a thought-of card in half a second, and finish with a cards-and-rubber-band-in-the-hands-of-the-spectator trick as a finale.

Moving on to walkaround and mingling, I recommend that you have a few good opening lines, some coins, rubber bands, and a deck of cards as a minimum. I've found that if you offer people who say they did magic as kids the chance to try something, and they need a coin or whatever, you can just bring it out and let them have a go. They look stellar no matter if the trick works or not, and you're the best there is. I think our job isn't to perform magic nonstop during the time we're booked. We're there to make the most out of the time we have with the audience. It can be spectacular to let the audience do something, so let them!

I usually open with a funny line, introduce myself as I pull something from someone's ear, and move on to make it all about them. I ask questions and take a genuine interest in what they're saying, and then I move on to some more magic. I share the story about my grandfather, and a joke about having been pregnant with twins and how that made my magic so much easier — I could hide *anything* behind me.

You don't need a lot of routines. Think of using three to four per group of people, and remember that some of that should be changed after moving to a new group. If someone, or everyone, watched the show from the side, it would be better if they got to see a full new set of effects. Let's say you do three effects per round, and you have three different sets, so you need nine effects in total.

If people are standing with a cocktail or something, and there are no tables, it's tough to ask them to help with the effects. So, before you get to the event, make sure you know how the room will be furnished.

If you're looking to add just a few short effects, I want to use the Swedish phrase *slå ett slag för*, which in a literal translation means "punch a battle for," but it really means "give a suggestion" for these effects: the pen behind the ear, coin in a pen cap, anything with a rubber band, that spooky little baby hand gimmick you put on your pinky, omni deck, and loops.

I've been handed a sponge dong too many times, and let me tell you: It's not funny in a formal setting such as a corporate party. Don't do it. And don't give me the whole "But Caroline, it fits my style, and people love it" BS. Just trust me on this.

Stage

I love stage magic! Some may argue that my material is more parlor, but it does the trick (ha) onstage just fine for me. My show is much more about me connecting with my audience than having big props to fill a stage. My personality fills it up just fine.

For cruises, I have two different 45-minute shows, and when I put them together years ago, I started that journey with my favorite hack: Post-its on the wall.

I wrote down every trick I knew, tricks I had but hadn't rehearsed yet, stories I liked to tell, and ideas for pieces I would perform to music. I put them up on a big blank wall. They all got graded with As, Bs, and Cs on them, and all Cs were instantly eliminated.

The As were my absolute best tricks, with an amazing script and well rehearsed. I divided those into two and went on to my Bs. The As would be the A-game material in both shows, and the Bs would be add-ons. I didn't have to add too many Bs, so I was very pleased with the outcome.

I use this exact process every time I write a new show or public speech, and I used it even when planning the contents of this book. I highly recommend that you try this method.

For my corporate stage shows, I usually perform a 25-minute show. Sometimes, during corporate dinners, they ask me to do a split show. I do one effect and some comedy after the first course, and the rest of the show after the main course.

My current setlist as I'm writing this book is this:

- Emcee introduces me
- Upward Rising 2.0
- Hug/Kill
- Sheer Luck

- Vanishing Water with a Spectator
- No Brainer

Please be inspired by this list and don't copy it. I'm sharing this to help you see how a show can be put together and not to give you a blueprint. Thank you for your integrity!

Charity Events

Every year, I set a budget for how much money I'd be okay skipping to help charities and organizations by performing for free. Of course, it's never "for free"; there's always a cost someone has to pay. When I'm not being paid with money, I'm the one paying with my time. When I accept a charity event, I'm doing that while being aware that I won't be able to take on any other work during that time.

My yearly budget for that is $30,000, meaning I can do an average of eight charity events per year.

How and if you decide to do charity events is totally up to you. I only accept when it's a charity or organization I believe in, or when I know I'll get excellent press or photos from it. At the end of the day, you're running a business, so find ways to be compensated for your services, even if it's not in the form of a paycheck.

The venue and caterer often get paid. If there's a photographer there, make sure you get the pictures and that the organizers properly thank you for sponsoring the event. I ask for this to happen four times: in the invitation, on the stage during the event, in the thank-you letter after the event, and on social media during the event.

Take a moment to think about what charities and organizations you'd like to support. You can wait for them to reach out to you, or even better, go out and create relationships and offer to help.

Another reason to do charities is the people they usually attract. High-end charities will attract wealthy people who go to events and parties. They will eventually need entertainment, so this is a perfect opportunity to showcase what you do.

Custom/Personalized Shows

My show is my show. When you book the show, that's the show you'll get — most of the time. Hear me out.

Some clients think it's vital to get their message across or to bring a specific person up onstage to do something special during the show. Of course, I can and do offer that, but most of the time, I or my agent remind them that the show is created this way and will give them the best outcome. I've performed my show as is so many times, and if it's not low-season, it's multiple times per week.

Having a tight show that you know will kill every time (I mean, all of us have bad shows, but you know, kill 99% of the time) is a good place to be. Selling something that solid shouldn't be difficult.

However, the client wants what the client wants. If they want me to mention their product, produce the CEO, or include the theme of the event, I usually present it as a tailored show, and there's an extra cost to it. If it's something simple they want, like me drinking from their cup or having balloons with their branding onstage, I don't mind it at all. But when it comes to personalizing a show, and you're looking at spending hours developing the material specific for them, it has a fee.

For years, I offered it for free and was so eager to please the booker — sometimes so eager that the show suffered from it. Do yourself, the audience, and the booker a favor: Be prepared and deliver the best job possible. Everyone will look better that way.

If you woke me in the middle of the night, I could still perform the show as it's written. If you did the same thing, asking me to add something from a specific client, I would know exactly where to place it in the show for maximum impact.

There are now two slots during the show where I can easily incorporate messages and special requests, free of charge if it's small. I usually charge an extra $500 to personalize the show to fit only during that event.

This won't sit well with everyone, but it has worked great for me. During busy seasons, I can do the show I do best, and if I have to work overtime and create something custom, I'm being compensated for that.

Public Speaking

Most working magicians are great performers. Not all, but many. Some of them are best sitting down, some have amazing silent acts, and some bring down the house with comedy. Many have more stage time than most, and telling compelling stories is what we do. We take out an ordinary object, tell a story, and add a magic effect. So, why not do public speaking?

In general, the money is better for public speakers. You'd be working most of the day, and you could still do evening events.

I'm having a hard time wrapping my head around why more magicians and entertainers don't do public speaking. You could, and probably should, include magic, and if you try the Post-it method I mentioned before, I'm sure you can get an outline for a lecture/talk in no time.

If you have a few ideas or concepts you could talk about, you might be sitting on a gold mine!

If you want to increase your credibility as an entertainer/magician or public speaker, look into TEDx talks. A TEDx talk is a presentation, lasting 15–18 minutes maximum, of you sharing an idea worth spreading. And that's the key to your submission: ideas worth spreading.

What's your big idea or take on something in this world? How can you add your personality and magic to that and share it with the rest of us? That's where you start, and keep your Post-its close!

Residencies

During my first year in business, I managed to land a residency at a pub. It was terrible pay, far from home, hard work, and worth every minute. The owners were happy, I was happy, and the visitors were even happier. We called it Magic Thursday.

Having a residency might sound fancy and fabulous, and it could be. But for most, it's nothing more than a regular paycheck. That can be very important while starting, or to have as a backbone of your business. If you're trying to sell your first offer as a resident magician, you might want to compare it with hiring a band. A band plays for everyone and interacts very little with the customers. A magician interacts, talks, and performs personally for the tables. It's a much more intimate experience – and most people have never experienced magic before, especially not done in their own hands!

Magic Thursday was my only steady income then; the rest was me relying on clients to magically find my number and call me about an event. Even though it wasn't a long contract, I learned many important lessons.

One thing I took away was that you only get really good at something if you do it hundreds, if not thousands, of times. The other big thing for me was how to introduce myself when approaching people who have no clue who I am or what I want.

I booked loads of corporate gigs from my residency, too. That was all about me showing the value I provided and them seeing it in action, both at their table and throughout the venue when I performed.

Part of the pay I got was in the form of food, and that seems to be common.

Cruise Ships

As mentioned before, you'll need a lot of material to start booking cruise shows as a guest entertainer, or GENT, as we're usually referred to. Remember: The standard is usually two completely different 45-minute shows and sometimes an extra 20-minute show for a variety of shows.

What I love about cruise shows is both the diverse audiences and the fact that I get paid to see the world. I usually perform one to two nights per cruise on a regular contract. The cruises I go on are one to two weeks long, so I have a lot of time to explore.

Before your show, you are as anonymous as you want. You can hang out by the pool, in the bar, in port, or do whatever you want, and not a soul will bother you. After the shows, you're a rockstar with all the perks that go with it!

Most cruise lines book their GENTs through booking agencies. I'm very fortunate to be working with an agent who used to do a lot of cruise shows as a GENT herself. That makes it easier for me to bring new ideas to her and to help negotiate the best possible contract for me. I'm being well taken care of while on board, and that's part of the contract they have negotiated.

After the cruise show is booked, the agency or its travel experts make my travel arrangements. Sometimes, I have to fly in a day before, but for contracts on the other side of the planet, I need two days of travel. They sort the flights, hotels, and most transfers.

If you want to go out and do cruise shows, the best way to book something is by finding an agency that books them. I work with Don Casino, and so far it's been a perfect match for me.

Emcee/Toastmaster

Ah, my favorite of all low-hanging fruits for entertainers! Embracing the role of an emcee, host, or toastmaster of an event offers many benefits beyond just a nice paycheck. Let's delve deeper into what this role means and why it's not only financially rewarding but also, at least for me, more creatively fulfilling.

First and foremost, being an emcee or host allows us to showcase our personalities and charm in a way that may not be fully realized during a typical walkaround or stage performance. While walkaround magic and table-hopping have their charm, often the interactions are brief and limited to small groups. Onstage, the magician may wow a larger audience, but as an emcee, the magician becomes the face of the event, the guiding force that sets the tone and keeps the energy flowing throughout the proceedings.

Imagine being the master of ceremonies at a prestigious gala or a corporate event. You're not just performing tricks; you're setting the ambiance, engaging with guests, and weaving magic seamlessly into the evening. Your presence becomes natural, and your wit and charisma leave a lasting impression on everyone present.

Also, as the emcee, you're granted the opportunity to establish rapport with the audience on a deeper level. Unlike a fleeting encounter during a walkaround performance, you have the luxury of time to connect with individuals, building anticipation for magic effects and creating moments of genuine wonder and awe.

The role of an emcee often involves improvisation and quick thinking, skills that are invaluable for any magician. Whether handling unexpected situations with grace or effortlessly segueing between event segments, the experience gained from hosting can enhance one's performance skills and overall stage presence.

However, the most rewarding aspect of being an emcee is the sense of fulfillment that comes from being the glue of the event. You're not just a hired entertainer; you're an integral part of the festivities, contributing to the occasion's success and leaving a lasting impression on organizers and attendees alike. If you aim to make the event as important to you as it is to the client, you're on the right path.

While the financial benefits of being an emcee are certainly enticing, the opportunity to showcase your talents in a more interactive setting makes this role appealing for many entertainers. So the next time you're offered the chance to host an event, don't just see it as another gig; embrace it as an opportunity to shine bright and leave a lasting magical impression on everyone fortunate enough to be in your presence.

Trade Shows

The exciting world of trade shows, where magic mixes with business in the coolest ways! For magicians, diving into the trade-show scene can be like finding a pot of gold at the end of the rainbow. Let's discuss why trade shows are many magicians' wet dreams and how you can do them, too.

First, trade shows are magnets for people. Attendees flock to booths like bees to honey, eager to check out the latest and greatest. The companies that book a spot are likely looking for ways to bring loads of leads to their booth. Your amazing magic tricks can stop attendees dead in their tracks and make any booth the talk of the town.

You'll want to customize your performances to fit the vibe of the event and company.

And let's not forget about the networking opportunities! As you work your magic at the booth, you'll meet all sorts of folks – decision-makers, influencers, and potential clients from all walks of life. A killer performance at a trade show could lead to some significant gigs or partnerships down the road. I would therefore encourage you to make it easy for them to find you afterward.

Plus, trade shows are the perfect playground for honing your skills. You'll learn to adapt to different audiences, perform in all kinds of crazy settings, and think on your feet when things don't go as planned.

Weddings

For most people, their wedding is the biggest day of their lives. Well, you might argue that it's when the firstborn arrives.

Some think you shouldn't do a *show* during a wedding, but I beg to differ. One reason against it is not associating the magic with the wedding and having that as the highlight. The bride probably wants her dress or the dinner or the first dance to be the most memorable thing about the wedding, not the magician who just showed up for a quick hit-and-run show. I'm not married, so I don't know. As I said, I don't agree.

A magic show during a wedding absolutely has a place. The earlier, the better, though, because many weddings serve a large amount of alcohol, and that makes it harder to keep your audience focused.

I've found that the best time to do walkaround is after the ceremony, before the dinner. During dinner, there are usually speeches that need to fit into the schedule, and I'd like to think that when I get married, my guests will be talking among themselves between courses, and an uncle will say something.

I've also been hired a lot as a toast madame during weddings, and it's the same as being an emcee at a corporate event. The only difference that matters is that at weddings, people often decide to spontaneously make a speech, and you're on a tight schedule.

Lost-Luggage Show

Honestly, I wouldn't feel good about publishing a book about how to make a living as a magician and not mention this: I've lost my luggage three times. Once, it sucked loads, once it was stressful as hell, and once, it was devastating. Choose your poison there.

What I've learned from these experiences can be boiled down to two very practical pieces of advice. The first is just one word: AirTags. However, no AirTag in the world will do you much good when you land in Seoul to join a cruise and your bag is stuck in Shanghai.

The second is: Have a backup show for when this happens. For years, I've traveled only with my carry-on, a backpack, and a men's suit holder. In my carry-on, I have all the things I need for my show, including printed cue sheets and a USB with all the music files and PDFs. My backpack is stuffed with makeup, clothes, and my laptop. The suit holder carries two pairs of shoes, two suits, and three to five dresses – but don't tell anyone!

My Lost-Luggage Show has become my cruise material. I don't let my bag out of my sight. If I'm going on a longer contract, I usually check a big bag with only clothes and shoes, but for the most part I have what I listed above. There are good laundry possibilities on the cruises too, so I'm not worried.

Make sure you have a backup for if something goes missing, and keep an extra setup of the show somewhere safe.

Repeat Bookings

There's nothing quite like the joy of knowing that your clients loved your performance so much they want more and are asking you to come back. Staying in contact is a great way to get repeat bookings, and there are a few clever ways you can do that:

- **Stay in touch:** Send a heartfelt thank-you note or email to the client after your performance, and follow up later to check in and see if they have any events coming up where you could work your magic again.
- **Create a newsletter:** Start a mailing list and keep your clients in the loop with regular newsletters specific to past clients. Share updates on your latest tricks and performances, and let them know if you've been in the news. Keep them engaged and excited for you and your success.
- **Get feedback:** After your performance, ask your clients for feedback. What did they love? What could be better? Show them that you value their input because it helps you improve and tailor your future performances. This is a great way to have real conversations to extend beyond a simple "thank you." If they say something that you later incorporate, send them a video or picture of it and thank them for the excellent feedback. Another great reason to connect!
- **Stay active on social media:** Share behind-the-scenes glimpses, provide client testimonials, and engage with your followers. I've noticed that I get more requests when I post about my shows a lot, and share different aspects of the show. This can inspire a past, or new, client to think of something that you'd be perfect for.

- **Offer a "finder's fee":** If a client refers you to another event or potential customer, why not give them a finder's fee for it, just as you would with an agent? I've done that quite a lot and it's been really good for getting repeat bookings within the same industry.

Test different ways and see what works for you, but the main thing I can tell you is simply to stay in touch. People are busy, but usually delighted when the awesome magician calls them in the middle of the day.

Part Four
Social Media

I'm currently on all the big platforms except Pinterest. It doesn't make sense to me to spend time there, but I'm sure you could find a reason for it if you really wanted to. You will figure out where you decide to be present along the way, but it's a good idea to try them out to see what fits you the best.

I divide my social media into A and B priorities. The A category includes the ones I'm on daily or weekly with *intention*, and B is generally for whenever I have time or something to share. That said, B is still one of my priorities. There was a C list, but it's now been deleted completely to avoid overwhelm.

My A priorities are Instagram, Facebook page, YouTube, and TikTok. I post daily on Instagram, Facebook, and YouTube Shorts, and I upload multiple new videos to TikTok and YouTube each week.

My B priorities are the newsletters, LinkedIn posts, and my platform. My platform is where I share topics like the ones in this book. It contains exclusive videos, live streams, and blog posts. My newsletter goes out weekly or biweekly, depending on the season. LinkedIn gets about two to three posts on good weeks, depending on my current workload.

When I run out of ideas, I turn to other creators, ChatGPT, and Answer the Public (see how below) for inspiration.

Know Your Audience

Who are you trying to attract to your business and brand? Depending on who these people are, sometimes just knowing their age and gender, you're probably looking at different platforms.

For corporate entertainers, LinkedIn will be the best place to share about what you do and who you help. Videos are best for visual platforms such as YouTube, Instagram, and TikTok. All social media platforms have different strengths and generally attract different crowds.

One thing I can say about them all is that consistency is key. The best way to grow on any social media platform is to tailor the content to what's the "norm" on the platform. Think about how users consume content on different platforms. You might want to publish the same photo on all the platforms that allow pictures, but they each have different preferred dimensions.

Regarding videos, some platforms use a vertical format, and some are better horizontally.

A general recommendation is to have a business account on any platform that allows it. It will look much more professional and authentic. It also allows you to access analytics on your profile to see your audience's engagement.

In the following chapters, I'll break down the different platforms and give you an idea of how you can leverage their potential. If and when you decide to be on multiple platforms and upload multiple times a day, it's smart to have a scheduling tool in place. I'm currently using Metricool, but before going with them I was using Later for years. It's a great service that I think is worth considering if you want to have a drag-and-drop solution. However, Metricool provides better analytics.

When you have multiple platforms that you want your audience to get to easily, you can add something called a Link in Bio or a Linktree. This allows you to share just one link with your fans; they decide where they want to go from there.

LinkedIn

Oh, I hope you change your LinkedIn game after reading this book! Sure, I could say "If you only take away one nugget, let it be this" for most of the book's content, but if you're not killing it on LinkedIn already, it's time for a change.

How much money do you make on Instagram/Facebook/TikTok/YouTube per month? How many hours do you spend in total on those combined per month? Or even per week or day? Most phones will tell you how much time you spend on each app, so have a look and challenge yourself a little.

For most readers, no money is currently being made on any social media platform. You might be getting some YouTube ads money here and there, and that's fantastic, of course, but there's a better way to spend your time.

What if you spent time connecting with people on LinkedIn instead of the doom scrolling you usually do multiple times daily?

LinkedIn isn't just for corporate professionals; it's a powerful platform for entertainers looking to expand their reach, connect with other entertainers, and create new opportunities.

You want to ensure that your profile reflects who you are as an entertainer and showcases the highlights of your career. Use a professional headshot, and write a captivating headline and a compelling summary that shows your unique talents and experiences. Remember that USP we talked about earlier?

There's a feature on LinkedIn that not enough users take advantage of, and that's the featured section. This is the perfect place to "pin" or "feature" your favorite articles, pictures, or websites so that they show up in your profile. Put your best work here, and feel free to change the featured posts occasionally.

Social media is social, but LinkedIn is more about the connection. So, when connecting with people, be strategic.

Connect with other professionals in your industry, including event planners, fellow entertainers and magicians, and entertainment agencies. Going the extra mile would be personalizing connection requests to establish a genuine connection. Adding some spice to the request messages will make you stand out!

Share updates about your performances, projects, or industry insights. Regular activity keeps you on the radar of your ideal clients and shows that you're actively involved in your field. You'll establish yourself as an industry leader – and that's exactly the place to be.

If you connect with people who have seen you in action, you can send out a request for them to give you a recommendation. Positive testimonials add credibility to your profile. The more recent the recommendation, the better. Make it a habit to look for opportunities to get a review anywhere you can.

LinkedIn is a fantastic place filled with business professionals. By being active and engaging on the platform, you can create many new and exciting gigs. Be genuine and generous. Spark inspiration!

Instagram

For me, Instagram is at its finest when storytelling meets engagement. When something is very compelling, the user stops to consume, read, and save/share/comment on what you have to say. It can be a short story, a piece of advice, or something pretty to look at, but if your audience isn't engaging with it, you're probably not doing it right — yet.

Think of content like spaghetti. If it sticks to the wall, it's done. If the content sticks with the audience, in this case by getting them either commenting, sharing, or engaging in any other way, it's finished and good! If not, it wasn't right for the audience and needs more time to cook in your brain.

If you want to up your Instagram game and basically any other platform really, here's how you can do so in a week.

Day 1: Define Your Instagram Strategy

Take the time to define your goals on Instagram. Identify your target audience, the vibe you want to convey, and the key messages you wish to communicate. Your Instagram profile should reflect your brand personality.

Day 2: Optimize Your Profile

Ensure your Instagram bio is compelling and concise. Add a profile picture representing your brand, and include a link to your website or other relevant platforms. Use keywords to make your profile easily discoverable.

Day 3: Content Planning

Create a content plan for the upcoming week. Consider a mix of posts, stories, and reels. Tailor your content to showcase your unique talents, behind-the-scenes glimpses, and engaging stories. Aim for variety to keep your audience intrigued.

Carousel posts are great for activating engagement, so people can scroll through the post to see the next slide.

Day 4: Engage with Your Community

Start engaging with your existing followers and relevant accounts. Respond to comments, like photos, and follow accounts aligned with your niche. Building a community involves active participation on your part, too. Don't be someone who "posts and ghosts," meaning just posting and leaving the platform. Instagram, and every other platform, wants all users to be active on their platform. Commenting on others' posts, being active in DMs (direct messages), and using all available features on the platform will help you build a community on every platform.

Day 5: Master Instagram Stories

Share a mix of spontaneous moments, announcements, and interactive content such as polls or quizzes. Instagram Stories provide a more casual, real-time connection with your audience. I aim for at least five stories every day.

Day 6: Utilize Hashtags Strategically

Research and identify relevant hashtags for your business. Use a mix of popular and niche-specific hashtags in your posts to increase discoverability. When someone searches on Instagram, Instagram wants to help the user to find the perfect content for them. Using hashtags and locations when posting helps the platform know who will benefit from your content.

Day 7: Analyze and Adjust

Head to Instagram Insights to assess the performance of your content. Identify the type of posts garnering the most engagement. Use this data to refine your strategy for the upcoming week. Based on your insights, experiment with posting times and content formats. If you're starting out, it'll take some time to get the right insights at first. Stay consistent and evaluate your performance as you move along.

To take this one step further, you can collaborate on posts to make the content show up on multiple accounts. Let's say you're sharing a video performance of someone's trick. You can tag them in the post and send an invite to collaborate. When and if they accept, the content will show up on their feed, too, making it visible to their audience as well.

YouTube

YouTube is like a massive stage that lets magicians and entertainers perform for audiences all over the globe. You can share your skills on all platforms, but YouTube is made for long-form content, making it the perfect place for you to show off your unique style and abilities – and publish your showreel.

As your channel grows, so do the chances to make money on- and off-screen through ad placements, channel memberships, sponsorships, and even paid gigs to bring you into events.

Sure, it's good to be spontaneous, but planning parts of your videos can help keep things smooth. Figuring out how to start, transition, and end your videos can make them look more professional. Don't forget to have great video and audio to up the production value. YouTube is very competitive, so if the audio or video isn't great, most users will drop out to watch someone else's video.

To attract more viewers, make your thumbnails and titles catchy and click-worthy. Using the right keywords can also help more people find your videos. YouTube is the second-largest search engine in the world, so making videos that people are searching for is a great way to get started. How-to videos are huge.

Interact with your audience by chatting with them, answering their comments, and making them feel part of the channel's overall purpose. You can ask questions during your videos and continue the conversation in the comment section.

Starting a YouTube channel takes time and effort, but with some (or a lot of) patience and practice, it's a great way to showcase your work and personality. Think about how you use YouTube and Google to find answers to your questions. If you're an expert in your field, people will come to you for answers.

When you grow as a YouTuber, you'll notice that different add-ons make the videos better. I've partnered with Epidemic Sound for years, which provides royalty-free music and sound effects. Many companies offer this service, but I've been very happy with the diversity of the sounds and with their customer service. As I said, I've partnered with them, so I get paid to share my experience when I share my affiliate link.

Facebook

Facebook has a user base of billions across all demographics, interests, and locations. For business owners and entertainers, this means unparalleled access to diverse audiences hungry for what we offer. Whether you specialize in closeup magic, stage illusions, or mentalism, Facebook provides a platform to showcase your talents to a global audience. The way you can target your ideal customer and audience is the most accurate approach I've ever come across.

To maximize your use of Facebook, tailor your posts to suit your unique style and audience preferences. Facebook is still one of the most-used social media platforms and allows us to experiment with different content types. How do you use Facebook? Whenever I'm unsure how to use a platform for my business, I turn to myself and a few friends to see how we usually spend our time and attention.

Think of Facebook as a thriving community where magicians can connect with fellow performers, enthusiasts, and potential clients. It's a great place to build a fan base. By joining magic-related groups, participating in discussions, and sharing valuable insights, magicians can foster meaningful connections, gain industry insights, and even collaborate on projects. Having your own page or group is an excellent extra step in using features on the platform.

I highly encourage you to look at Facebook's advertising tools. Whether promoting upcoming shows or showcasing testimonials from satisfied clients, Facebook advertising offers a cost-effective way to boost our brand presence and attract bookings. I went on a national tour a few years ago, and I only spent $250 in ads to sell out all the shows – all on Facebook. One of Facebook's greatest strengths is its ability to have direct communication between entertainers and fans in multiple ways. From responding to comments and messages to hosting interactive Q&A sessions and live performances, Facebook is the perfect platform to engage with our audience in real time, enhancing a sense of connection and loyalty.

A well-maintained Facebook presence conveys professionalism and credibility. By having a polished profile, regularly posting content, and responding to messages, you can position yourself as a trusted expert in your field, earning the respect and admiration of your audience.

The way I personally use Facebook the most these days is for the magic groups and promoting upcoming shows. In my business, I use it to upload videos, pictures, and stories, share testimonials, and stay connected to my fans.

TikTok

To understand how to use TikTok, I would start by using it for a few weeks to get an idea of how it works and what the different features do. It's a platform where you need to grab the viewer's attention quickly.

At its core, TikTok is about a vibe and getting as many views as possible. Building numbers for followers and views is easier here than on any other platform. Easier, but not easy. As I've mentioned, it's all about knowing your audience and how to feed their hunger. If TikTok is not for you, you don't have to use it. The same goes for all platforms, of course, but remember that a TikTok is the same as a YouTube Short or an Instagram Reel. If you're not excited to be on TikTok, there's no immediate need to be there.

Most consumers of the content on TikTok are young, trend-savvy people looking to fill their entertainment needs in seconds. They want bite-size content that doesn't have to tell much of a story to be good. It is all about the visuals, designed to keep it appealing and make it stand out.

When TikTok arrived on the scene, it was all about riding trend waves to get views and followers. Many magicians have used TikTok to share quick tricks, and even to reveal how the tricks work by having someone stand behind the magician who's performing for the camera. Most effects are ruined for the spectator when doing something like this, so they come in as a stooge/actor. This has worked great for many magicians! Some use the platform to gain millions of followers by sharing how tricks work. How ethical this is, I'll leave up to you.

Like all other platforms, TikTok requires consistency to be able to grow. The more you immerse yourself in the TikTok culture, the better you'll understand how to get clicks, views, and followers. The bigger your TikTok is, the easier it is for you to monetize on the platform with brand deals. This is also true for all the other platforms.

Creating compelling content takes time, and all platforms are different. You can always add more platforms as you develop your online presence.

The group that uses this app the most is still young people up to the age of 35. Of course, these people can be your target audience, but there are better platforms if you're looking to book corporate gigs. However, going on tour requires butts on seats.

Long-Form versus Short-Form Content

Long-form content pillars are usually podcasts, YouTube videos, and livestreams. We've discussed videos before, so let's move on to podcasts. One way of becoming an industry leader is to be the host of a podcast. Here are a few ideas that might be for you.

Share magic theory and insights on different principles. For instance, the listeners could ask questions about certain topics on Instagram, and you give a long answer in the podcast. It could vary from explaining sleight of hand to discussing the psychology of magic.

You could interview other magicians to let them tell their stories and share valuable insights. The topics might include creativity, stage presence, or memorable moments in their careers. Business advice for entertainers could also be included.

Another idea would be to educate listeners about the history of magic and great magicians from the past. There have been loads of very successful and influential magicians, and I personally would love to listen to a podcast like that.

To make this short-form, you could use quotes from the podcast or even snippets of conversation. Include these in a reel or story, or even transcribe them into a carousel post. Let your imagination guide you. You could also record your podcast with video and upload that on YouTube.

Short-form content is more bite-size. It can be short videos like TikToks or reels, photos, or blog posts. As mentioned, you can use your long-form content to create short-form. What I've done a lot is create a YouTube video about something and then publish a short blog about the same thing. Then, I send that out in a newsletter and promote the YouTube video. Furthermore, I can use a piece of that blog as a caption on Instagram and Facebook posts.

Answer the Public

My favorite go-to tool for content ideas is AnswerThePublic.com. It's a powerful online tool that provides insights into what people are searching for on search engines such as Google and YouTube. It's like a window into the minds of internet users, giving you a glimpse of the questions and topics they're curious about. It's as if you're reading the minds of your audience in just one click.

When you enter a keyword or topic into AnswerThePublic.com, it generates visualizations of search data in the form of word clouds and lists. These visualizations display the common questions, prepositions, comparisons, and related terms that people are typing into search engines. This means that you'll get the exact phrase that your target audience is searching for.

This information is invaluable for content creators, marketers, and anyone looking to understand their audience better. By knowing what questions people are asking, you can tailor your content to address their needs, interests, and concerns effectively. You'll be able to answer questions they haven't yet asked by understanding what a typical search from a target audience member would look like.

Whether you're brainstorming ideas for blog posts, YouTube videos, social media content, or website copy, AnswerThePublic.com can provide you with valuable insights and inspiration to create content that resonates with your audience. This process has saved me countless hours, especially for blog posts and YouTube videos.

One strategy I use a lot for YouTube is to answer very specific questions. To know what my ideal customer or viewers are asking, I type my general idea into AnswerThePublic.com, and it will show me the questions that need answering.

The free version lets you do three daily searches. This is an excellent way to get started, but I've bought a lifetime subscription since I use it so much.

Tips on Filming Yourself

Something I'm sure you've come to understand by now is that I use my devices intentionally. The Apple Watch is one of my favorite tools to use on shows to get extra videos and pics taken when I'm out alone.

Put your iPhone on a tripod or against a wall/chair/object. Open the camera app on your Apple Watch. See your frame on the Apple Watch. Press record/take a pic when you're ready. If you take away nothing more from this book than just that life hack, I'm happy I could do that for you! You don't need someone to come along to shows. Pics and videos are great for social proof and will be a good investment when it's time, but you can do a lot just with your phone.

Please clean your camera lens beforehand. In fact, do it now. Just rub it against your shirt. Right before the show starts, clean it again to get the best possible shot.

Part Five
How to Book Gigs

It's finally time to start looking at how to book gigs! As you've come to understand by now, there are a lot of things that come into play when booking a gig.

We're magicians and artists, and we usually start our business journey in the opposite way to entrepreneurs. This could be where the expression "starving artist" comes from.

Our journey usually looks something like this:

> I'm a magician, and I'm great! I love to do magic, and therefore people will book me. I'll sit around and get really good at my craft; then I'll be rich and famous. I'll create a show of effects that fooled me and that I can afford, then place them in a random order. Ta-da!

An entrepreneur usually starts by identifying a need and seeing potential buyers. Where do these people gather? The businessperson then sells the solution to that problem – in our case the magic show.

Coming at it from an entrepreneurial perspective, our journey would look like this:

> Clients are having events. I'm a magician, and I'm great, so I will reach out to them and offer to help them with

> their message and entertainment. My show is crafted so that the clients' unique themes or pain points can be addressed during the show.

I listened to an interview with some of Red Bull's marketing minds a while back. In the interview, they mentioned that they don't portray the actual product in the advertisements but rather the feeling it provides. They said they don't show the product because that's not what they're selling. They show the logo, yes, but they also share the adventure that comes after drinking a Red Bull. That's their story.

If we're selling a solution for a problem, which we are, we should tell the story of what happens when clients hire us. It is a real skill to put their problems into words and to showcase a solution they can pay for without being "salesy."

I've also found that the more people who know that you do magic for money, the better. Everyone knows someone who's going to an event. When you network, make sure to let people know that you're a magician. You have to go out and meet people, present an offer, and pitch yourself. The more people who know that you trade magic for money, the more times you'll be considered and contacted to do a show.

Showreel

We did cover videos when talking about foundations, but this needs one more chapter. If you don't have a showreel and depend on people talking about how good the show is, you won't be in this game very long.

If you want to make it easier for a client to understand what your show is and what the overall feel during the show is, you need a good showreel to demonstrate that. If you're doing different types of shows, you're going to need different showreels. Make each one as unforgettable as you can.

The most crucial part that needs to be included is you doing what you do on a stage and an audience that's hyped about seeing it. You will go further by adding social proof such as testimonials and a list of past clients – the bigger the names, the better! The more over the top the showreel is, the better. Show only your best parts! People are busy, and their attention span is sometimes nonexistent, so keep it short. Kill your darlings and have sharp scissors.

I've seen so many bad showreels, and some of the worst contain talking-to-the-camera parts that are terrible (please don't talk to a camera if that's not a skill you actually have), lousy editing, and terrible audio. If the audio for the clip you'd like to use is bad, add music on top. If you're not good at editing, there are many editors to be found online. Look at Fiverr or ask in a magic forum on Facebook. That's where I found my YouTube editor.

Your First Paid Gigs

When you start booking gigs and getting out there to test your wings, you're not going to be exceptional. And that's okay!

You can and will book your first gigs without any of the fancy stuff that I mentioned in Part One: Foundations (even though it's all basically mandatory in the long run). You won't need to have your website up or high marketing budgets.

Start simple and ensure you're comfortable performing the effects you decide to do. No magician or any other professional started out great, and you're not going to either. Know that in advance and set a small fee to reflect your current level. The client needs to be happy with what they have, especially if you want a testimonial to use later in your marketing.

With your business plan in the back of your mind, you'll know what the benefits of having you at the event are. You know your USP and market. The best way to get most things is to ask for them. If you can be convincing in your attempts to show the benefit for the client, it's easier to land the gig.

Local charity events are another great place to look for some stage time. Comedy clubs, improv nights, and openings for someone at an event could also be good options.

And just a quick note on pricing: Being the second cheapest on the market has no market value. If you're new to performing at paid events, don't make other magicians race you to the lowest price. It's not doing anyone any favors.

Add value; don't be an extra cost your client didn't plan for.

Networking

Networking is key for most entrepreneurs aiming to make a full-time living from their craft, no matter what it is. By connecting with the right people, magicians can secure more bookings and opportunities – mainly because you can ask what people do and what they're planning and then offer to help. But it's not just about meeting people; it's about nurturing those connections and actually networking. Have you ever heard the expression "Your network is your net worth"?

Think of networking as planting seeds. You need to follow up and water those seeds to see them grow. Don't give up too soon! Send referrals their way and keep the conversation going. Help them any chance you get.

Understanding the customer journey is crucial. From the initial inquiry to securing the booking and even after the gig, maintaining client relationships is essential.

One effective way to network is by joining professional networks and communities such as BNI (Business Network International) or local TEDx events. These networks provide opportunities to meet like-minded individuals and potential clients. Remember, people buy from people, not just companies. Building relationships is key to success in any business, and the magic business is no exception.

When attending networking events, make a memorable pitch and ensure you leave a lasting impression. Take the time to connect with everyone you meet, exchange contact information, and follow up afterward. I love having a reason to get back to people about stuff. It can be anything. One of my favorite ways is to talk about something I saw/read and then go, "You know what, you'll love it. I'll hunt it down and send it to you!"

Networking isn't just about getting bookings; it can also lead to unexpected opportunities. For example, one magician landed a lucrative partnership with a booking agent who increased the yearly income for that magician by 400% in one year simply by performing at a networking event. Oh, that magician is me.

So, don't underestimate the power of networking. Take the time to build relationships, attend events, and seize opportunities. Who knows what magic awaits?

When talking to people, remember that most people love to talk about themselves. My most commonly given advice in all areas of life is to ask more questions than you reply to. The key here, though, is to ask questions that will produce a positive and energetic answer.

Side note: I got a sponsored car out of networking. A striped Mini Cooper. I had no driver's license at the time. Long story – ask me when you run into me.

Sales and Lead Generation

I'd like to briefly walk you through a standard process of sales using the textbook 7-step sales process.

This is just an outline, and the following steps provide a good summary of what you should be doing to find potential customers, close the sale, and retain your clients for repeat business and referrals in the future.

Step 1: Prospecting

In this first step, you look for potential clients. You look for people or businesses that need what you have to sell – and make sure they can afford what you offer. This process is known as "qualifying."

Depending on what your offer is and what you charge for it, you can't stop at just one prospect per company. It's said that, on average, there are 6.8 customer stakeholders involved in making a typical purchase in modern sales.

My services usually require me to reach just one or two people per company, but most of the time, they're part of a party committee. It's rare that one single person makes a decision there and then. In fact, I can't remember the last time that was the case for me.

Step 2: Preparation

Now that you know who to contact, you move on to the next phase, where you start preparing for an initial contact. This includes researching the market and collecting relevant information regarding your product or service.

Take your time to prepare a sales presentation and tailor it to the potential client's needs. This is a key part of your success with this. The better you can understand the needs of the client, the easier it becomes to address their objections. This will set you apart from most of your competition.

The client doesn't want to be sold something. They want to be understood and to make intelligent decisions. Make it easier for them by being prepared and always being on their side. You're here to help!

Step 3: Approach

At first, it can be scary to approach a client. Remember, if you have an amazing offer and have a solution for their need, you've come a long way.

There are multiple ways to approach potential clients. You can email, call, send a DM (direct message) on any platform, or have a face-to-face meeting. There are three common approach methods:

- **Premium:** Give them something at the beginning of your interaction. In my case, I like to invite them and a partner or co-worker to a public show.
- **Question:** Get the prospect interested by asking questions. This is the approach I use in my cold emailing or DMs.
- **Product:** This involves giving them a sample or a free trial to let them evaluate whether the service is for them. I'm sure you have taken part in this many times. It could be accepting a beverage on the street or trying out software for 14 days. Basically, anything where they get a taste of what it is.

Step 4: Presentation

Typically, this step would imply using a PowerPoint presentation, and can be very salesy. You can demonstrate your offer in many ways. Be creative! No matter the tools you use for the presentation, always make sure to be listening actively to your customer's needs. Act and respond accordingly. At times, you're not the best fit for them, and that's okay. Remember that you're trying to help them, and you could always refer them to someone else. (More on referrals later.)

Step 5: Handling Objections

This step is the most underrated step in the 7-step sales process. This is when you put your biggest ears on, listen to the prospect's concerns, and then address them.

Many salespeople drop out at this point. I've seen different numbers for this, but most of the sources I've checked are saying that roughly 44% abandon their approach after one rejection, 22% after two rejections, and 14% after three. After four rejections, 12% abandon the attempt. Do that math really quick and gasp at the fact that 80% of sales require at least five follow-ups to convert.

Successfully handling objections and concerns separates good salespeople from bad, and great from good. Don't give up too soon.

In my experience, selling my magic show or services as an emcee takes two to five tries. It's different when the client reaches out themselves, of course. If you're not a famous person or known to be the best in your field, many times they're shopping around. They might have been put in charge of the entertainment for the Christmas party, and that's a big deal! They might be looking for the cheapest option and nothing else. But if you do step 2 right and can reply with an understanding of their needs, you're going to stand out from the competition. Many just reply with a fee.

There's no strategic advantage in being the second cheapest in the market, and you'll hear me say that again.

Step 6: Closing

At this stage, the client will decide whether to proceed. There are a few different closing techniques, and depending on your business, you might find one that works or try all three.

- **The alternative:** Assume the sale is done and offer them a choice where both close. "Will you be paying in full upfront or in parts/installments?" Or "Will that be cash or card?" I use this technique on my kids all the time! "We're leaving in a few minutes. Would you like the green or the blue shirt?" I'm not much for bragging about my parenting skills, but with this, I close 99% of the time.
- **The extra inducement:** Offer something extra to get them to close. It can be very effective to add a free month or a discount. It could also involve adding an extra service. For example, you can offer to do an extra 5–15 minutes of something. This is how I started doing emceeing. It was something I wanted to do but didn't have experience in, so I wasn't comfortable selling it as a service – yet. Win, win.
- **Standing room only:** With this close, you create urgency in the decision-making process. That can be that the price will go up after today, we only have five spots left, or that someone else is asking for the same date that they wanted. Scarcity and urgency can be very effective, but I've found that this can also drive the client away, especially if they have a large group of decision-makers for the offer.

Step 7: Follow-up

Yay, you got hired and got the sale! That's great news, but your work doesn't stop there.

Knowing how long it can take and how pricy it can be to go through the process of acquiring a client, it's worth nourishing the relationship. It's important to get this step right for both potential repeat business and referrals.

In this step, I also ask for references and if I can share my experience working with them on LinkedIn. This gives me another reason to reach out again, sharing the blog or post with them.

Cold Outreach Strategies

The thought of cold calling or emailing venues might seem intimidating at first. The good news is that there's a simpler, more effective approach: tapping into your personal connections at first. So that's where you should start looking.

Think about your network. Maybe you know the owner of some bar or restaurant, or your friend's spouse manages a conference center. These connections might not seem immediately relevant, but they could serve as valuable entry points to getting gigs. Think of who you know and who they know.

Every chance you get, let people know that you do magic in exchange for money. If they don't know this, how would they know they can hire you for an event?

Now, let's talk about cold email outreach — a powerful tool for getting your foot in the door. I've personally found LinkedIn to be an invaluable resource for identifying professionals who might be interested in booking entertainment for their events.

Here's an example of a cold email template that I've used successfully:

> Hi [name],
>
> I recently came across your profile on LinkedIn and was intrigued by your role at [company]. My name is Caroline Ravn, and I've been a professional magician for over a decade, specializing in corporate events and private parties.
>
> I'm reaching out to see if you have any upcoming conferences or kickoff events where my magic could help make the occasion even more memorable. I've had the pleasure of performing for [mentioning notable clients

I've had recently that match their market], and I would love the opportunity to bring some magic to your event as well.

If you're interested or would like to learn more about my work, feel free to visit my website at www.carolineravn.com. I'm always happy to chat further about how we can collaborate to create an unforgettable experience for your guests.

Looking forward to hearing from you!

All the best,
Caroline

By personalizing your emails and showcasing your unique skills, you'll increase your chances of catching the attention of potential clients. And remember, persistence pays off – follow up with your contacts to keep the conversation going and stay on their radar.

So, start mining your network for opportunities, and don't be afraid to reach out to potential clients via email. With a bit of creativity and perseverance, you'll be well on your way to securing more gigs.

Showcase

If you have good videos, pictures, and testimonials of your offer, you have a solid foundation to stand on when booking shows. Well, assuming you have a good show already, of course.

I've done a few showcases in my career, and they are hit or miss, really. If you don't know what a showcase is, it's basically you doing part of the show for potential bookers. Where I've seen the most success is me performing for booking agencies.

When doing a showcase, only bring your absolute A game. Remove all the fluff and filler material you have, and as much of the in-between talking as possible. Be tight and prepared. It's great if you can see the venue before, so make sure to arrive before the audience, just as if it were a corporate gig.

Expanding upon the importance of showcasing your magic effectively, let's dig deeper into successful showcases to land gigs.

Showcases serve as invaluable platforms for magicians to demonstrate their talent directly to potential bookers, whether they're event planners, venue managers, or booking agencies. However, the effectiveness of a showcase can vary significantly depending on various factors, including preparation, presentation, and audience engagement.

When preparing for a showcase, meticulous planning and attention to detail are paramount. Begin by curating your repertoire to showcase your most captivating and visually stunning magic tricks. Consider the demographic and preferences of the audience you'll be performing for, tailoring your act to resonate with their tastes and expectations.

Furthermore, it's essential to streamline your performance, focusing on your strongest and most compelling routines while eliminating any fluff or filler material. Keep the pacing dynamic and engaging, ensuring that each trick leaves a lasting impression and builds anticipation for the next.

In addition to refining your act, investing in high-quality promotional materials such as videos and photos can significantly enhance your showcase presentation. A professionally edited video reel showcasing highlights of your performances, accompanied by striking photos capturing the magic in action, can captivate potential bookers and leave a memorable impression.

When it comes to the showcase itself, timing is crucial. Arrive early to familiarize yourself with the venue and stage setup, allowing ample time for any necessary adjustments or sound checks. Consider the logistical aspects such as lighting, sound quality, and audience seating to ensure optimal conditions for your performance.

During the showcase, strive to maintain a strong connection with the audience and command their attention from start to finish. Engage with spectators, interact with volunteers, and inject your personality into the performance to create a memorable and immersive experience.

It's also essential to be adaptable and responsive to the audience's reactions, adjusting your performance accordingly to maximize impact and resonance. Pay attention to cues and feedback, and be prepared to improvise or modify your routines as needed to keep the audience engaged and entertained.

Finally, follow up with potential bookers after the showcase to express gratitude for their attendance and inquire about their feedback or interest in booking your services. Personalized follow-up emails or calls can demonstrate professionalism and reinforce the positive impression you made during the showcase, potentially leading to future bookings and collaborations.

In conclusion, showcases offer magicians a valuable opportunity to showcase their talent and secure bookings, but success hinges on meticulous preparation, engaging presentation, and effective follow-up. By mastering the art of showcasing your magic, you can elevate your visibility, expand your clientele, and advance your career in the competitive world of entertainment.

Money-Back Guarantees

Some entertainers offer money-back guarantees. I know a few magicians who do, and it is completely up to you how you're going to go about this.

I've done this work professionally for a long time, and only once did it ever come up – in a tiny format. There was a client who was not 100% happy, and I could (and should) probably write a book on only that topic at some point because the takeaways from it were insane, but I ended up removing a percentage of the fee instead.

I don't think you need a money-back guarantee, but if something happens, I think it's good practice to allow the client to be right and meet them at a reasonable place. That's going to be different for each client. In my case, as I said, it made sense to lower the fee they paid.

Referrals and Testimonials

Imagine this scenario: You're considering booking a magician for your event. Naturally, you turn to Google to find the best fit. What's the first thing you look for? Personally, I look for someone who has excellent reviews. Like me, my potential clients are scouring the internet for social proof that I'm the real deal.

When sending out emails with offers and updating your website, you want testimonials that paint the picture of how great you are. The louder someone else shouts this message, the less work you have to do. But where do you get them?

As mentioned before, don't be shy about asking for reviews. Start by reaching out to friends and family; they're probably your biggest cheerleaders and will be happy to support your journey. Write a friendly email or message asking them to leave a short testimonial on your Google Business profile or website.

Another strategy I've used in the past is to capture testimonials on the fly. Keep your phone or camera handy after your show or performance, and when audience members compliment you, seize the moment! Politely ask if you can record their kind words, and *voilà* – you've got authentic, spontaneous testimonials ready to be shared with potential clients.

People genuinely want to help people they like. If they loved the show, they're very likely to say yes to this.

Booking Agencies

Joining a booking agency could be the key to unlocking a world of opportunities and expanding your reach as an entertainer.

First and foremost, clarity is key. Before approaching a booking agency, take the time to define who you are as a magician and what sets you apart from the rest. What makes your magic unique? Why should clients choose you over other performers? Having a clear understanding of your brand and value proposition will make it easier to communicate your strengths to booking agents and potential clients. Did you finish your foundations? Good, let's move on then!

One of the most significant benefits of working with a booking agency is gaining access to a wider audience. These agencies often have extensive networks and connections in the entertainment industry, allowing you to reach clients and venues that you may not be able to access on your own. By leveraging the agency's connections, you can secure more bookings.

Videos are essential tools for showcasing your talent to potential clients, and booking agencies are no exception. Invest in high-quality promotional videos that highlight your skills, personality, and unique style of magic. These videos serve as powerful marketing tools and can help booking agents pitch your act to clients more effectively.

As I've said, testimonials are another crucial component of your promotional toolkit. Collecting feedback from satisfied clients and audience members can help build credibility and trust with booking agencies and clients alike. If the booking agent has never seen you before, it can be a big help for them to see what other clients have said in the past. This will also help them know which audience of theirs you'd be the best fit for.

Flexibility is key when working with booking agencies. Be willing to offer different packages and options to accommodate the needs and budgets of various clients. Whether it's a 5-minute kickoff performance or a full-length main act, having a range of options available will increase your chances of securing bookings and satisfying clients' needs.

Part Six
Becoming a Pro

As you've come to understand throughout this book, there's a lot that goes into "becoming a pro." It can also mean different things, depending on your goals and skill set.

For me, being a professional magician is much more of a lifestyle and choice than I thought at first. Running a business is hard, but I love its challenges. Being onstage, landing a big contract, and talking to someone cold thrills me. I even get excited talking about other acts if I'm not able to take on an opportunity myself.

For this chapter, I'd like to walk you through a normal year for me and many other entertainers. Let this live rent-free in the back of your head as you embark on this journey. Or, if you've been around for a while, this is a good reminder of the different seasons that usually look the same year in and year out.

The First Year in Business

This will be the year of "putting it all together." You'll get your photos taken, build a client list, write and rewrite your business plan, and practice your pitch more times than you ever thought possible. You're going to learn an insane number of skills that will help you throughout the rest of your career. There's no reason for me to sugarcoat this for you. It's going to be challenging, and you're going to get a lot of "no"s.

I like to think of "no"s as something good. It means we're not a great match now, but it doesn't have to mean we'll never be a good fit. I take the "no"s and make them into relationships. Embrace the "no"s and learn from them. Was it something in the pitch or the offer? Didn't you understand the client's needs enough?

In the first year, you're also going to establish a more professional online presence. That means LinkedIn, Instagram, and your website, for example. Talking to agencies and building copy for socials and newsletters. Let it take time and try to be an early adapter of a mindset of "How can I repurpose this?" Say you create a newsletter about an upcoming show. How can that idea for content also be a LinkedIn post or two, Instagram reels, and a blog post? Be creative and use your time wisely.

Attention is the most valuable asset we have. Why should someone switch their attention from something else to spend time on your platforms? The earlier you understand this, the better.

I would recommend you set up Google Ads early on, too. If you're not great at this, it's worth hiring someone to help you with it. Knowing who to target, how much to spend, how to use negative keywords, and much more is a jungle. You'll be busy enough, so if this is not something you already know about, or it doesn't excite you, leave it with a professional.

Take the first year to build a solid foundation for yourself and your business. Develop an early habit of reaching out to people.

After three, six, nine, and twelve months, look back and see what worked and what didn't. I see many performers making the same mistake for years, so don't let that be you.

So, what does the first year in business usually look like? It's a rollercoaster ride of highs and lows, late nights and early mornings, victories and setbacks. You'll wear many hats – CEO, marketer, accountant, and more – as you navigate the challenges of entrepreneurship. But through it all, remember that every hurdle is an opportunity to learn and grow. And to have fun!

A Typical Year as a Magician

Let's break down a typical year for me and many other magicians.

- **January:** Very slow. Possibly an event here and there, but nothing major. Most big companies have just had a Christmas party, so there is no immediate need for entertainment.
- **February:** Same as January, but usually bigger shows and budgets.
- **March:** Corporate galas and events start happening again. Loads of emceeing/hosting events and after-dinner entertainment.
- **April:** Same as March.
- **May:** Better than March and April, and also adding on some summer parties and BBQs at the end of May.
- **June:** Summer parties mainly. Weddings are also popular here, of course. I usually do cruises from June to early September, maximum.
- **July:** Cruises for me, but many magicians do private parties and weddings at this time.
- **August:** Still weddings, but from mid-August the corporate shows start up again. This is usually in the form of kickoff parties and conferences.
- **September:** Gala dinners and conferences mainly.
- **October:** A lot of corporate parties and events. Usually conferences and award dinners.
- **November:** Early November is like October, and then mid- to end-November marks the start of Christmas parties.
- **December:** For many, me included, exclusively Christmas parties of different sizes.

Usually, things get booked one to three months in advance. Before the pandemic, it was more like three to six months in advance. I've seen this change for all aspects of events, so not just us entertainers. It's for catering, venues, and everything. If you want to pitch for a show, look three to four months in advance and see what might be a good fit for you. It's better to start building a relationship early and nourish that until it's time to book the upcoming event. It's always good to be top of mind, so build a strong relationship.

Building a Team

The most people I've ever had on my team was 16 people at the same time. This was in 2018 when I was on a national tour with my show, *Where the Magic Happens*. I was the only one onstage, and usually only my agent Charlotte came with me to the event, but I had a whole team of people helping with the tour. Some were on a payroll, and some got paid in burgers and beers – literally.

It's never been my intention to go on this entrepreneurship journey alone, nor go on tour alone. There's so much power in working with people who want to see you succeed. It doesn't matter how great a performer you are; looking for just this one person or this one opportunity to change your entire life is unrealistic. Usually, you'll need a bunch of different people coming in at different times.

Today, I have a full-time assistant who comes to the office and comes with me to shows when I need her to. I have two main agents, and I'm listed with loads of booking agencies. Out of those, there are about eight to ten agents who book me regularly.

When do you add people to the team? The easiest and most general advice I can give you is simple: as soon as you can afford to. It doesn't have to be someone full-time. It can be hiring someone from Fiverr to edit videos, someone who creates your website, or a Google Ads expert.

Hiring people isn't just a financial decision. This is where I see a lot of business owners get this whole thing wrong. It's an attention and time decision. It's an investment. Let's say you're struggling with social media management. You could spend hours trying to craft the perfect Instagram post, or you could hire someone who's an expert in the field to do it for you in a fraction of the time. Time saved is time earned.

Learn to buy back your time and energy by working smarter. Reach out to schools for interns, collaborate with friends, or hire freelancers. The key is to surround yourself with people who complement your skills and share your vision.

I've been fortunate enough to work closely with individuals who have transformed my business for the better. Each person has played a vital role in my journey, from agents to editors to interns. And trust me, once you start building your dream team, you'll wonder why you didn't do it sooner.

Establish Niche Authority

Being a magician is pretty "niche" already, and being a popular one in a small country like Sweden is very lucrative. However, I want to stand out and be the obvious choice and the best possible investment for my clients. Therefore, I've spent a lot of time becoming an authority.

When I was 28 years old, I set a goal of doing three TEDx talks by the time I was 30. I ended up having done five by the age of 31. Now I can say everywhere that I'm a five-time TEDx speaker, and that's not only super-impressive but also builds a lot of trust in me as a stage personality. This has landed me more gigs via LinkedIn than anything else. People see my profile and instantly know that I'm a safe bet if they don't already know of me. It makes me credible.

If you don't know anything about TEDx, it's an independent event under the umbrella of TED. TED stands for Technology, Entertainment, and Design, and their entire idea is "ideas worth spreading."

It's worth mentioning that TEDx doesn't pay you to participate. They might cover flights and hotels, but you'll get a video with their branding. If you stick to the time frame, they'll share it on their website, too. Did I mention the credibility it comes with?

So, how can you secure a spot on the TEDx stage and establish yourself as an authority?

Identify your superpower: Reflect on your unique skills, experiences, and perspectives. What sets you apart from others in your field? How can you captivate and inspire an audience?

Choose your topic: Select a subject that you're passionate about and feel confident discussing. Your enthusiasm and expertise will shine through, captivating both the audience and the TEDx organizers. For most entertainers, we don't really need a "topic," but more a red thread. It depends what you're going for, of course.

Network with organizers: Connect with TEDx event organizers and volunteers through platforms like LinkedIn. Express your interest in speaking and inquire about upcoming opportunities. But before that, offer to help them in any way you can. Maybe volunteer at an event and become part of the community.

The pitch: Make sure to highlight your unique perspective and the value you bring to the TEDx stage. Let the organizers see your passion and expertise, demonstrating why you're the perfect fit for their event. Usually, a TEDx event has a theme. If possible, use the theme in the pitch.

The talk: Most TEDx events have dedicated speaker assistants who will help with the talk or performance. I've found that I personally like a talk that starts in the middle of a story and builds from there. Look at what others have done and see what draws you in. Remember "ideas worth spreading."

Balancing Life and Business

I love my job. You probably know that by now. I love performing, running my business, and building fans and relationships. All that is great, and I also love my family.

To me, having a "balanced life" means that I get to live both lives at the same time. I can still be the GENT on cruises, and I get to be a mother. I can stay home with my kids when they're sick, but I can also stay an extra day in Vegas if I need to.

I think this can be a long and hard conversation to have with family members if you're used to being someone who always goes to work at the same time, but I met my partner after I had already been doing this job full-time for six years. There was really nothing to discuss about the fact that I had to go away to work. However, when I got pregnant (before we knew it was Double Trouble), we had a conversation about how the upcoming years would be organized. We decided that a priority that works for our family is the following:

- **Priority 1:** My shows
- **Priority 2:** His business (he's also an entrepreneur)
- **Priority 3:** Everything else on my to-do list.

Having this planned out beforehand has saved us so many fights and misunderstandings. I don't know how helpful the above list is, but if there's anyone reading this who wonders how I manage it all, that's how. That, and the fact that we had a nanny for the babies' first year.

Celebrate Wins

Did you call someone cold, and it went okay? Great – celebrate! Did you sell out a national tour? Great – celebrate! Make it a habit to always find things and achievements to celebrate.

The best thing about having a team of people around you is that you always have someone to celebrate with. It can be just a call and a virtual high-five, or bringing the whole team out for burgers and beers. I've found that celebrating wins is a way of living. I do this in my professional and personal life.

In fact, I do it so much that I now have small bottles of champagne in my fridge with notes with goals on them, so I'm always ready to celebrate when the goal is achieved. And I don't even like champagne! It's more the act of celebrating. The act of acknowledging that you did something you decided you wanted to do and went through with it. Like this book! When it's 100% done and shipped out, there's a bottle ready to be opened in my fridge.

This whole chapter links back to your goals and whys. Have a good look at them again and search for achievable milestones so that you can easily know when it's time to uncork that bottle.

I'm known among my friends to celebrate twice. I celebrate when I get an amazing opportunity and then again when it's achieved. The champagne doesn't come in until the end, but it's nice to always live in a positive state of celebrating successes. Sometimes, being considered for an event is worth as much as actually booking the event. Not financially, but emotionally. Knowing that your foundation and your offer were so good that it's considered for that amazing event is a great feeling. Sending an invoice afterwards is also very rewarding, but not everything.

Part Seven
Adding Value

Even though this is the shortest part in the book, it's packed with invaluable knowledge. What you're about to read on these next few pages is responsible for more revenue than anything else in my business. With that said, I hope you're ready. Brace for impact, and read it twice!

The Value

You come with superhero capabilities and experience that not many have in the room you enter. You can move people into a world where anything is possible, and yet, sometimes, there's no room in the budget.

Offering to add value to the potential client can look different in different situations, but I'd like to explore some of my favorite ways to help them help themselves. Remember that you are in a need-fulfillment business.

What skills do you have that are not the magic show you pitched? Maybe, if you're doing kids' parties or family events, you could offer to do balloon swords or dogs for the kids at the end. Do you know some simple face-painting figures? Could you offer to help share the event on social media or LinkedIn?

Where are the people your client is trying to attract? Is it an open event like a charity event, and they want to reach a broad audience? You could offer to do a trick on your social media channels where you perform a trick with a script that explains what the event is and ends with an invitation. All this can be part of the extra value you can bring to the client.

Overdeliver and show that you care about the success of their event more than what ends up in your bank account. If you're looking to get rich fast, or even get rich at all for most of us, you're in the wrong business.

My go-to for adding extra value to my clients is offering to host the event at the same price I quoted for the show or adding an extra 15 minutes to the VIPs or executive board members. I would go that extra mile and shuffle my deck of cards a few more times to ensure my client is getting the best value for hiring me, not my competitor.

If you're willing to roll up your sleeves and drop your ego to be a helpful partner and trusted advisor, you're more likely to get the gig than others. Most magicians send a quote and wait for the client to accept, and nothing more.

If you're really serious, you have to keep in mind that "business" is the longer word in "show business" and that you're an entrepreneur offering a service to assist in a project much bigger than you.

If that's you, congratulations! I'm sure you'll see a lot of success in your business, whether you're planning on doing this part-time or full-time.

Part Eight
Making Extra $ as a Magician

I've been doing this long enough to be comfortable with what a year as a performing magician looks like. It has ups and downs, and you usually know about the seasons for different shows in advance.

Looking at other income streams can help you stay mentally calm and manage the stress of not having gigs booked.

Passive Income

Making money as we sleep sounds too good to be true, but that's exactly what passive income means. There are many different ways to make passive income, and my favorite (and most lucrative) methods are mentioned here.

For a few years now, I've consulted for other magicians on their shows and businesses. Consulting is active, but after pinpointing the main issues magicians are having with their business, I've created a course helping them with all aspects of their business. It's this book but on crazy steroids.

I've done a lot of paid collaborations, where I post a video or photo once and then get paid for clicks or subscriptions. I was the hands for McDonald's France, for instance, and I got paid for the days we recorded. Every year they use the materials, I get royalties. Pretty sweet deal!

Before I had this big transformational beast of a course mentioned above, I sold smaller courses for beginners and semipros. I recorded them once and then reaped the rewards for years.

Membership sites are great for generating passive income, too. There are many different ways to do it. Instagram Subscriptions and Patreon are popular memberships. I used to be on Patreon, but since then, I've created my own platform at www.ravnmagic.com, where I share in-depth tutorials and business advice and host exclusive livestreams. I see it as a site for the VIPs, the hardcore fans! They have a special place in my heart and get news before anyone else.

As a YouTuber, I also get paid for my videos every month. Videos I published years ago are still generating money monthly. A little tip on how to make videos that keep on giving is to answer very specific questions and make them evergreen.

So, talking about topics that people will need the answers to for years to come.

I also have loads of merch, such as clothes and playing cards, but that's a whole other chapter.

Affiliate Marketing

Recommending products and getting a kickback if someone purchases that product is known as affiliate marketing. To track if you're getting a click or sale, it's usually connected to a specific link and, if not, a promotion code.

I personally only work with brands that I love and use myself, but part of being an influencer can mean teaming up with brands you've never heard of. My main platforms for pushing affiliate links are YouTube and my newsletter. Whenever it's an affiliate link, I try to mention it as clearly as possible. It doesn't come with any extra cost for the customer, so I get a cut from the sale directly from the company I teamed up with.

I have a few different brands I work closely with, and the two that are the most lucrative for me are Amazon and Epidemic Sound. You don't need a big following to get started on these, especially Amazon. You sign up to be part of Amazon Associates, and whenever you recommend a product, you share an affiliate link in your caption or description. It's usually a very small cut you get from recommending Amazon products. It's 1–20%, but most are under 5%. There are thousands of videos on YouTube on how to do this, so if you're interested in how it works and want to see all the steps, I'd recommend you go there.

For Epidemic Sound, it's a little different. I get paid 50% of the subscription fee when someone signs up. That's very generous and generates a hefty sum every month. In the previous chapter, I mentioned that I have videos that make me a lot of money, and the ones on Epidemic Sound are at the top of that pyramid.

I think of affiliate marketing as a way for me to get paid for talking about products and services I already love and use. When brands reach out to me that I've never heard about before, I either turn the collaboration down or ask for an extensive free trial to give it an honest review for the sake of authenticity.

Merch and Online Shops

In 2015, I teamed up with the incredibly talented founder of Stockholm17 Playing Cards. Our first meeting was at a pancake place, and he showed me over 15 different design ideas for what came to be known as Ravn Playing Cards. I loved them all! As of writing this book, we have 11 different decks accompanied by mini-decks, coins, and all sorts of merch that has been shipped worldwide.

Deciding on where to sell merch and which company to trust with clothes is a jungle, but for years now, I've been pleased with Threadless for all apparel. The quality is good, and they have reasonable pricing and shipping times. They also run promotions on autopilot. All I had to do was upload all my designs to the platform in a transparent PNG format, decide on which layouts I wanted, and then the platform did the rest. However, the sales happen when I actively promote the products. Threadless is a free platform, but it earns a commission on sales. Since it's a print-on-demand service, I don't have to worry about storage.

For Ravn Playing Cards, I've tried it all, basically. Now, I use Shopify and Gambler's Warehouse to ship everything out. I never touch it! Shopify comes with a cost, but it has been great for this part of my business. Since all my Ravn Playing Cards have been founded on Kickstarter, I never had to pay out of my own pocket to have them printed. It's been a really nice source of extra passive income for me.

I recommend Canva for templates and inspiration if you want to start creating merch.

60+ Ideas for $

After touching on different ways I make money, other than when I'm performing, I'd like to share a long list of ideas for you to consider. Maybe some of these can help you reach higher revenue. Look at your entire skill set. Is there anything you enjoy doing? Are you really good at something? How can you incorporate magic into it? This list is not even close to complete, but I hope it sparks inspiration for you.

Physical Products:

- Big magic sets
- Single tricks
- Gift bags
- Birthday party add-on package with everything from invites and thank-you cards
- Balloons and pump for balloon sculpting
- Playing cards
- Wands
- Closeup mats
- Books
- Lecture notes
- Unique playing-card displays
- Coins
- Gimmicks
- Clothes
- Paintings and art
- Prop building

Services:

- Balloon animals
- Face painting
- Renting out party supplies like bouncy castles and chairs
- Promoting other magicians and entertainers for a fee
- Lectures
- Consulting
- Commercials
- Hosting events and parties
- Workshops
- Emceeing
- Public speaking
- Light and sound design with technical riders

Digital Products and Services:

- Guest writer: Writing on someone else's platforms can be a great way to spread the word about who you are and what you do. Some will charge for you to market yourself on their platforms, but it's just as common to get paid to share ideas.
- Writing for newsletters
- Writing for magazines
- Writing for blogs

Ebooks:

- Tips and strategies for advancing in the competitive world of magic
- How to grow an audience: strategies for magicians to build a loyal fan base
- Building a brand: techniques for creating a unique and memorable brand identity as a magician

- Growing your audience: insights on expanding your reach and attracting new followers as a magician

How-to Guides:

- Step-by-step manuals on mastering different classic magic tricks and techniques
- How to take better pictures of magic with your smartphone
- How to do flourishes
- Budgeting tools to help magicians manage their finances effectively
- How to network as a magician
- How to shuffle cards like a master magician
- How to cheat at cards
- How to please an audience
- How to increase engagement
- How to fill up a large stage with small props

Printables (Anything That Needs to Be Either Filled In or Ticked off):

- Business plan templates – comprehensive templates tailored for magicians looking to start or grow their businesses
- Accountability journals
- Weekly tasks and challenges
- Planners
- Content calendars filled with magic-themed content ideas for different social media platforms

Online Courses:

I've found that selling a course with one clear transformation is the best. Something with quick wins and a clear goal.

Templates:

- Sales copy
- Emails
- Posters and flyers
- YouTube thumbnails
- Content structure

Videos and Photos:

- Editing videos for other magicians (I have a magician who edits my YouTube videos, for instance)
- Lightroom presets

Business and Entrepreneurship:

- Sales funnel blueprints: strategies for converting leads into paying customers
- Step-by-step guides for launching successful crowdfunding campaigns for magic projects
- Tools and techniques for increasing productivity and efficiency for entertainers
- Tips and tactics for effectively marketing magic services and products
- Workshops and seminars to help magicians and entertainers develop leadership skills and grow their businesses (hit me up if you ever decide to host one!)

DIY and Hobbies:

- Crafting your own illusions
- Magic-themed toys and games that teach magic principles and tricks

- Entertaining and educational shows, on or off screen, that explore the world of magic
- Creative thinking workbooks for magicians

Final Thoughts

Don't quit too soon. Okay, thanks, bye!

No, in all seriousness, running a business is hard. It takes dedication and sacrifice. But at the end of most days, it's absolutely worth every drop of blood, sweat, and tears you could spare.

I've found that it helps to talk to everyone. Tell everyone that you're an event entertainer for hire. The greater the number of people who know this, the more gigs will come your way.

I hope this book inspires you to go out and chase your dreams. Use it as a reference guide, and thank me later.

BUSINESS
BOOKS

Business Books

Business Books publishes practical guides and insightful non-fiction for beginners and professionals. Covering aspects from management skills, leadership and organizational change to positive work environments, career coaching and self-care for managers, our books are a valuable addition to those working in the world of business.

Recent Bestsellers from Business Books Are:

From 50 to 500

Jonathan Dapra, Richard Dapra and Jonas Akerman
An engaging and innovative small business leadership framework guaranteed to strengthen a leader's effectiveness to drive company growth and results.
Paperback: 978-1-78904-743-1 ebook: 978-1-78904-744-8

Be Visionary

Marty Strong
Be Visionary: Strategic Leadership in the Age of Optimization
Demonstrates to existing and aspiring leaders the positive impact of applying visionary creativity and decisiveness to achieve spectacular long-range results while balancing the day-to-day.
Paperback: 978-1-78535-432-8 ebook: 978-1-78535-433-5

Finding Sustainability

Trent A. Romer
Journey to eight states, three national parks and three countries to experience the life-changing education that led Trent A. Romer to find sustainability for his plastic-bag manufacturing business and himself.
Paperback: 978-1-78904-601-4 ebook: 978-1-78904-602-1

Inner Brilliance, Outer Shine

Estelle Read
Optimise your success, performance, productivity and well-being to lead your best business life.
Paperback: 978-1-78904-803-2 ebook: 978-1-78904-804-9

Tomorrow's Jobs Today
Rafael Moscatel and Abby Jane Moscatel
Discover leadership secrets and technology strategies being pioneered by today's most innovative business executives and renowned brands across the globe.
Paperback: 978-1-78904-561-1 ebook: 978-1-78904-562-8

Secrets to Successful Property Investment
Deb Durbin
Your complete guide to building a property portfolio.
Paperback: 978-1-78904-818-6 ebook: 978-1-78904-819-3

The Effective Presenter
Ryan Warriner
The playbook to professional presentation success!
Paperback: 978-1-78904-795-0 ebook: 978-1-78904-796-7

The Beginner's Guide to Managing
Mikil Taylor
A how-to guide for first-time managers adjusting to their new leadership roles.
Paperback: 978-1-78904-583-3 ebook: 978-1-78904-584-0

Forward
Elizabeth Moran
A practical playbook for leaders to guide their teams through their organization's next big change.
Paperback: 978-1-78279-289-5 ebook: 978-1-78279-291-8

Readers of ebooks can buy or view any of these bestsellers by clicking on the live link in the title. Most titles are published in paperback and as an ebook. Paperbacks are available in traditional bookshops. Both print and ebook formats are available online.

Find more titles and sign up to our readers' newsletter at www.collectiveinkbooks.com/business-books

The Business Side of Show Business: How to Make a Living Onstage is the ultimate guide for performers who want to turn their passion into a sustainable career. Written by Caroline Ravn, an accomplished magician, emcee, and 5x TEDx speaker, this book offers a comprehensive roadmap for anyone looking to make a living in the performing arts – regardless of their niche. Caroline wrote this book to demystify the business side of show business, offering practical, actionable strategies to help entertainers build profitable careers on their own terms.

Packed with insights from her journey, Caroline dives into the critical aspects of running a business, including marketing, networking, pricing, and client relationships. From understanding the financial nuances of a performance career to mastering negotiation and booking strategies, *The Business Side of Show Business* addresses the questions many performers have but rarely find answers to. It's everything she wishes she knew when she got started.

Although written by a magician, this book is designed for every kind of performer or stage personality – from magicians to musicians, comedians to dancers – who dream of stepping into the spotlight and making a sustainable income doing what they love. With Caroline's guidance, readers will learn how to thrive as artists, entrepreneurs, and entertainers, building a career that marries passion with profit.

BUSINESS & ECONOMICS
UK £11.99
US $15.95

www.collectiveink.com/business-books

US $15.95
ISBN 978-1-80341-959-6

9 781803 419596